T4-AJT-149

WE TEACH THEM WRONG

WE TEACH THEM WRONG:

RELIGION AND THE YOUNG

by

RICHARD ACLAND

LONDON
VICTOR GOLLANCZ LTD
1964

First published May 1963
Second impression September 1963
Third impression May 1964

Printed in Great Britain by
The Camelot Press Ltd., London and Southampton

To Brian Badcock

"This," said Christ, "is life eternal, to know Thee, the only true God, and Jesus Christ Whom Thou hast sent," and this knowledge the men of the Dark Ages had in a degree which we, *who live in times when the Church is traversing the vast desert which separates the devout faith of the past from the baptised science of the future*, can hardly realise.

Frederick Stokes in an Introduction to Maitland's *Dark Ages*, 1889 (my italics).

CONTENTS

PERSONAL PREFACE

In the summer of 1955, when I went to Wandsworth School to ask for a job, I told the deputy head master that I was a Lay Reader in the Church of England and could perhaps help with R.E. lessons. His eyes sparkled; and I found myself landed with seven periods a week—one each with seven different forms. I attempted to plough through the relevant parts of the Agreed Syllabus; but the fact remains that I could not hold the boys' attention for five minutes; they did not even keep quiet. I had to ask the headmaster to relieve me of these religious duties.

Looking back, I think it might all have been different had I applied for a place as a One Year Senior Student in one of our training colleges. But it did not occur to me. My second-class Oxford degree allowed me to go to any school and offer to teach. I was anxious to begin; and pride and impatience won an easy victory over the wisdom and humility that might have accepted a year's delay. It was one of the biggest single mistakes that I have made in recent years; and I do not feel that I can start writing this book without confessing it. After all, the book may perhaps be read by one of the colleagues who tolerated me at Wandsworth despite the religious fiasco.

There is one other matter that I have to confess. I hope my case is not so bad as that of the prolific writer about whom they said: "Old George is writing his book again this summer." But I cannot disguise the fact that some of the ideas appearing in this book have also appeared in other writings of mine. In particular several sentences that I have read in the works of other writers have struck me, from time to time, with the greatest possible force; and I am not always going to leave those sentences out of the book merely because I have already quoted them in some other.

I am indebted, in all that follows, to so many people that I cannot begin to make a list. But it would be discourteous to go ahead without saying that this book could not have been written—not, at any rate, in anything like its present form—if it had not been for P. W. Martin, for his book *Experiment in Depth*,[1] his contributions to discussion in *Education for Teaching*, and above all for his leadership in a weekend's discussion course at Moor Park, Farnham, in July 1961. I must also thank several of my colleagues at St. Luke's College who have helped me with generous advice despite, in at least one case, considerable disagreement from my general position. It goes without saying that I am alone responsible for what is wrong in the following pages.

R. A.

Killerton,
Exeter.
July—December 1962.

[1] Published by Routledge and Kegan Paul.

CHAPTER ONE

IS ANYTHING WRONG?

IS THERE ANY evidence that anything is wrong with our teaching of religion as it is at present?

When I have talked about it to groups of teachers in Exeter, Leeds, Nottingham, Ipswich and other places in the last eighteen months, it has not usually been necessary to spend time convincing them that all is not well with our present performance of the duties laid on us by Section 25 of the Education Act of 1944. But then, my talks have usually been advertised under some such title as "What's wrong with R.E.?" And it may be argued that those who attend a lecture thus advertised are possibly drawn from disgruntled and unrepresentative minorities. Perhaps I ought not to start a book on the same theme without collecting two or three items of evidence to justify my anxiety.

Let us look at a book published by the Institute of Education at Sheffield University called *Religious Education in Secondary Schools*. Questions were set to 564 pupils in Modern Schools, 212 in Technical Schools and 457 in Grammar Schools, the numbers of boys and girls being in all cases almost equal.

Why do we keep Whitsun? 81% of modern boys, 70% of modern girls, 91% of technical boys, 71% of technical girls, 69% of grammar boys and 45% of grammar girls, did not know.

Name two prophets who gave their names to books in the Old Testament. 86% of modern boys, 72% of modern girls, 90% of technical boys, 71% of technical girls, 77% of grammar boys and 64% of grammar girls, could not do it.

The children were asked to number in the order of their happening, the Stoning of Stephen, Paul's shipwreck, the Last Supper, the coming of the Holy Spirit at Pentecost, and the

Conversion of Saul. This is not a very difficult question. It requires no such feat of rote memory as is involved, say, in recalling such a non-logical fact as that tangent = opposite over adjacent, sine = opposite over hypotenuse and cosine = adjacent over hypotenuse; one only needs to have a "feel" for the story as a whole and the events arrange themselves by necessary logical connection. But only 7% of modern boys, 16% of modern girls, 6% of technical boys and 9% of technical girls could get it right. On this question the Grammar Schools did appreciably better. Just over a quarter of the boys and just under a third of the girls gave the right order.

The children were asked to complete, with a name from the Old Testament, the phrases: ". . . *was a great Isrealite law giver*"; ". . . *is said to have written many of the psalms*"; ". . . *was famous for his wisdom.*" 66% of modern boys, 82% of modern girls, 86% of technical boys, 80% of technical girls, 61% of grammar boys and 60% of grammar girls, could not do it correctly. I find this one particularly shocking. After all, we are asking a question as simple as if, in history, we asked the children to complete: ". . . *burned the cakes*"; ". . . *signed Magna Carta*"; ". . . *had six wives.*"

Many other points were covered in this Sheffield research; but enough have been quoted to substantiate the conclusions of the authors:

> "The main survey clearly indicates that religious education in schools is making little impact on children. . . .
>
> "It is true that some of the results from the Grammar Schools are better than those from the Modern Schools, but they are not startlingly better. In many departments of religious knowledge there is little or no difference between them. This indicates that there is something wrong with the religious education given in secondary schools. If we cannot blame lack of ability in the children for unsatisfactory results, we must examine other factors; the timetable, the teacher, the syllabus, the scheme of work, and the subject matter."[1]

[1] *Op. cit.*, pp. 51 and 45.

My only critical comment upon all this is that I should have thought one might also take a look at the children and at life in the world where they live—which is what I propose to do in this book.

In July of 1961, the *Observer* published a feature article in which Arthur Barton made an attack on the whole teaching of religion in Secondary Modern Schools. It happened that I had just agreed to speak on this subject to a weekend conference organised by the Young Teachers' Section of the Devon Association of the National Union of Teachers; and I asked the organiser, when sending out notices, to send also a copy of Barton's article and a duplicated form asking teachers to express an opinion about it. This form was a pitifully amateur effort. The teachers who received it were asked to indicate by "tick" which of six possible opinions most nearly expressed their own view. The first three of these possible opinions, as will be seen, were critical of R.E. and favourable to Barton with decreasing emphasis; the last three were complacent about R.E. and critical of Barton with increasing emphasis. In detail, with the numbers of supporters after them, the opinions were:

Barton's description of R.E. lessons broadly corresponds to my own experience.	Six
Though Barton fairly describes a good many R.E. lessons of which I've heard, yet I hope and believe I get rather better results.	Nineteen
Though the overall situation is not as bad as Barton makes out, he gives timely warning of the direction in which we are moving.	Thirty-five
Though Barton may correctly describe the position in some schools, my impression is that the general state of R.E. in the "average" school is steadily improving.	Thirty

Barton's article is a serious exaggeration; in general R.E. is in a much healthier state than he suggests.	Twenty-eight
Barton's article is a complete travesty of the facts; there's nothing seriously wrong with R.E. at all.	Six

I quote the result of this trivial survey precisely because, at first sight, it seems to tell against me. Very roughly those who answer are divided half-and-half between pro-and-anti-Barton and between anti-and-pro-R.E. But one or two factors may lead one to revise this first impression. The forms were very often filled in by the R.E. teacher who was, in effect, being asked to criticise himself; the corrosive acids of modern life are likely to have eaten less deep in our rural Devon than in the great towns and cities where most of our children go to school; and a fairly high proportion of Devon teachers come from St. Luke's College from which, even if they do not leave as convinced Christians, they will mostly take a fairly solid respect for Christianity.

But, more decisively, I want to ask whether there is any other subject in the curriculum for which the same degree of criticism could have been expressed and could have commanded anything like the fifty-fifty support that is here shown for Barton's views. I quote below the most important sentences from his article with one modest alteration. Wherever he referred to religion, Christianity, or religious teachers, I have substituted, in italics, *maths*, *mathematics* or *mathematicians*. This is how his article then reads:

"Unfortunately, because there are so few practicing *mathematicians* about, *maths* specialists are hard to find, and where they exist their lot in the climate of opinion obtaining in schools today is unlikely to be very happy unless they are exceptional persons. Secondary Modern staff-rooms approximate to barrack rooms in freedom of language and forthright opinions, and I have seen several run-of-the-mill *mathematicians* whose narrowness (which isn't necessarily integrity) aroused some resentment among their colleagues and made their stays brief and unhappy.

"This lack of specialists leads to *maths* becoming the Cinderella of the curriculum. The necessary periods are farmed out among the staff and anybody may find *mathematics* on his timetable one or twice a week. . . . I know some who frankly use the lesson to teach their own subject. They get away with this because many headmasters are no more convinced of the need and value of *mathematics* than are their staffs, and turn a blind eye to the whole business.

"It is probably better to teach one's own subject *sub rosa* than to make a feeble attempt at teaching *mathematics*. . . .

"It would do *mathematics* no harm, and perhaps a great deal of good, if it could be cut right out of the State school curriculum, at any rate after the primary stage."

Who can suppose that such an article, if written, could have gained anything other than overwhelming repudiation from any random group of teachers in any county in the land?

Dr. J. W. Daines, of the Nottingham Institute of Education, submitted to just under 400 students at teacher training colleges, a questionnaire asking them to look back and comment upon the religious instruction they had at school; their replies relate, therefore, to what was done and not done in the top forms of Grammar Schools. Dr. Daines' conclusions are, in part:

"The evidence is quite clear that over a very considerable part of the field sixth formers are not receiving the help they need or deserve. . . . There is much evidence of something bordering on spiritual hunger in the desire to understand what religion is about and almost a pathetic need for a secure foundation upon which to build their lives. In far too many cases they appear to be receiving stones for bread and are left floundering with a growing conviction that it is all irrelevant anyway."[1]

[1] *An Enquiry into the Methods and Effects of Religious Education in Sixth Forms*, published by University of Nottingham Institute of Education.

F. W. Garforth, Lecturer in the Educational Department at Hull University, writes in *Religion and Education* (Spring 1961):

> "The writer's doubts . . . have been strengthened by his experience in interviewing candidates for admission to a training department; for when asked, 'Have you any comment to make on the way you were taught R.K. at school?' nine out of ten give a reply which is thoroughly depressing in its revelation of ineffective and unimaginative teaching."

Nor are the difficulties found only in the schools that are run by the community. Hugh Dickinson, the Chaplain of Trinity College, Cambridge, recently wrote an article under the heading: *Killing Religion in the Public Schools*. In the course of it he said:

> "Something like 60 to 70 per cent of men who have been confirmed at their public schools *arrive* at the university either non-communicants or avowed agnostic or sceptical. . . . Many boys still at school continue to conform to the accepted practices of the religion that has adopted them . . . although they are inwardly sceptical . . . and are known to be so by their contemporaries and juniors. It is not only after they have left school that we can see the weakness of the boy's religious and moral education. . . .
>
> "University chaplains are perturbed at the manner in which the intellectual and moral battles are already lost—or often going unfought. There is far too much naïvety about the arguments on which even intelligent schoolboys have rejected the faith."[1]

Naturally such a line of argument produced an outcrop of letters very largely from those who teach religion in the schools that were criticised. Most of them seem to have said, in effect: "It's not our fault, it's the homes", or "It's the fault of society as a whole". But taking education as a whole—in the school, in the home and in the wider community—hardly any expressed

[1] *Sunday Telegraph*, February 11th, 1962.

complacency. This state of affairs has been confirmed to me in recent months by close friends and relations who have just passed through public schools—not all of them at the less famous. Their general verdict: "You can take it that pretty well the whole of the sixth form is fed up with Christianity."

I shall add one further piece of evidence so as to bring us back to the schools in which the majority are educated. The headmaster in one of Exeter's Secondary Modern Schools generously allowed me to meet his fifth form once a week for the school year 1961-2, so as to take their R.E. period with them. The form consisted of seventeen boys staying on voluntarily beyond the statutory leaving age in the hope of passing O-Level examinations. One day, when they were getting to the end of a piece of writing that I had asked them to do, I wrote on the board: "What do you think of the story of Jonah and the Whale?" and asked any who had finished to write an answer while the rest completed the main task. At my request they were writing without putting their names on the paper; and here are some of the replies:

> "It is untrue, because a whale hasn't got a throat big enough to swallow a man; it couldn't eat a man because it hasn't got teeth."
>
> "It is a bit hard to believe, but possible. He would probably have suffocated. The story may have been distorted through the ages due to the changing of many languages."
>
> "I think Jonah and the whale is a lot of rubbish, *a whale has to digest his food like any other animal.*" (In this case the words in italics had been so heavily scratched out as to be decipherable only with the utmost difficulty.)
>
> "I think the story of Jonah and the whale could be true, but of course a lot would depend on the size and attitude of the whale and on whether Jonah kept calm."

Moved by these answers, I invited teachers whom I met at a small gathering in Taunton, to put the same question to any top secondary form with which they came in contact. As a result, I was able to read well over 200 answers. It is difficult, as anyone knows, to categorise a set of short essays; but I was able to divide them roughly in the following way: Twenty-one did not know anything about the story; twenty-seven merely gave their version of the facts without expressing any opinion; one hundred and twenty-five dismissed the whole thing as utterly impossible; twenty-three believed it because with God all things are possible; eight thought something like it may have happened and then been exaggerated; fourteen made some slight effort to deal with the story as myth or parable but yet involved themselves one way or another in an argument about its factual truth; fourteen (i.e. just under 6% of those who answered) firmly dealt with the story as a parable so that no question of its factual truth or falsehood could arise.

I was particularly moved by a grammar school girl who wrote:

> "When I hear anyone mention Jonah of the Old Testament I want to hide because I think his story leaves me wondering. . . . As a Christian who longs to help others to know Christ as I do, I feel that Jonah puts anyone off believing in God and miracles."

Why should this Christian girl be left in this distress? Why don't teachers stand up in their classrooms, and parsons in their pulpits, and stab their audiences into twentieth-century awareness by roundly proclaiming to them that there is not a single word of truth in the book of Jonah from beginning to end? Not a word of truth! No more than there is in Bunyan's *The Pilgrim's Progress*. There is no difficulty about this. Children of eleven and twelve can see at once that just as Bunyan wrote an allegory to convey profound religious meaning, so likewise did the author of the book of Jonah. And what a wonderful story it makes! A Jew in the fourth century B.C. had enough religious insight to know that his own people were deeply at fault in their narrow religious exclusiveness; and to know, too, that his words would be rejected out of hand if he directly told them that God cares for unbelieving foreigners as well. And so he invents his wonderful tale about God's call to Jonah to go and preach to the people of "Moscow". It is as well to say Moscow in the first instance because this word to our ears today has some of the same overtones as had Nineveh to the Jews of those days. I need go no further into the detail of explaining this inspired parable to any company of children. But it is not explained like this in our schools; it is not explained like this in our churches. And thus thousands of twentieth-century children are left to drift one step nearer to the point at which they will slam the doors of their minds against religion on the grounds that "a Christian is the sort of man who believes such rot as that a man lived three days in a whale".

As a matter of fact, my modest opinion poll on Jonah had an interesting sequel after I had discussed the results with a few of my friends. A day or two later one of them asked if I might be barking up the wrong tree because, as he showed from the volume he held in his hand, an author of a Biblical Commentary had been treating Jonah as inspired parable from at least as early as 1896.[1] But the book he showed me was a book written for scholars; and I am no scholar, and this book of mine has almost nothing to do with scholarship. I am to a small extent a teacher; and my book certainly has something to do with teaching. There is only one subject on which I claim expert experience, and that is *propaganda*. For nearly forty years I have carefully watched all kinds of propaganda—my own and other people's. And whether I or they have succeeded or failed in what we wanted to put over, I have tried resolutely to challenge the outcome with "Why did it succeed?" or "Why did it fail?"

My book is concerned with propaganda.

All who are directly engaged in propaganda, and plenty of other people too, are nowadays increasingly conscious of the word "image" as it is used by the Public Relations Officers who work for various organisations. We all begin to be alert to these images as they form themselves when we hear such phrases as "Southern Rhodesia", "British Railways", "The Conservative Party", "The B.B.C.", or "The Trade Unions". Such images may be sharp pictures seen by the mind's eye almost as clearly as I see a Low Cartoon in the *Guardian*. Or they may be

[1] *The Book of the Twelve Prophets*, by George Adam Smith (Hodder and Stoughton), pp. 494-500.

much vaguer—mere emotional feelings, almost sounds or tastes perhaps—and though they may move us powerfully, either by attraction or repulsion, yet we should often have great difficulty in describing them in words, or in suggesting the ways in which an artist might put them on paper.

Naturally the image of anything in anyone's mind will always be a severe simplification of that for which it stands; but it is important that there should be some kind of basic correspondence in quality between the one and the other. To take an example, it would be a pity if an unpleasant image were to form itself in my mind at the mention of "The Stock Exchange" if that institution, when understood in all its complexity, is a thoroughly healthy and necessary organ of modern economic life.

It would be an even greater pity if the images forming themselves in tens of thousands of adolescent minds at mention of "The Church", "Christianity" or "The Religious Way of Life" were to have little or no correspondence to the twentieth-century Truth. But this is, indeed, the very state of affairs which I think has been brought about by the great and recent changes that have come over our world, and by our failure, in classroom and in pulpit, to make the correspondingly necessary changes in our teaching methods. And I believe that enormous numbers of young people (and, for that matter, of middle-aged and old people as well) see and feel these false images, and reject them as repulsive or at least as irrelevant and unacceptable; and thereafter keep their minds barred and bolted against the Truth—unless, of course, something unusual happens to them.

It is very difficult to correct a false image, once it has been widely imprinted on thousands and thousands of minds so as almost to form part of the subconscious social background within which people do their conscious thinking. But it is not impossible. It ought to be attempted, and with courage and resolute persistence it could be done. But it would need nothing less than a revolution in our methods of teaching religion.

CHAPTER TWO

DO WE NEED A REVOLUTION?

NO ONE SHOULD lightly call for a revolution; not even in teaching methods. If we are to face anything so drastic, we must be shown good cause.

Clearly it is not enough to say that revolution is needed merely because our present teaching is not particularly successful. Nor is it quite enough to say that things are changing. This is always true; and anyone will agree that our teaching needs constant adaptation to meet the steadily changing outlook and vocabulary of our pupils as the social atmosphere of one decade gradually transforms itself into that of the next. If we are to entertain thoughts of anything that may properly be described as revolution, we must be convinced that something has been happening to us in recent times much bigger in scale, more decisive, more nearly unique than the persistent course of historical change within which men women and children have always lived, and always will.

Can we convince ourselves of anything of the kind?

In discussing this matter with groups of teachers, I have sometimes begun by asking about the hyphenated word "epoch-making". The Hollywood people, for example, never spend ten million dollars on a film without getting someone to describe it as epoch-making. This is rubbish; no film, not even Al Jolson's *Singing Fool*, has ever made an epoch.

How many epoch-making events, then, have there actually been in the whole course of human history? How many developments can truly be said to have ushered in a new epoch for the whole human race? The answer to these questions is: Two. And the second of these epoch-making events is now only in the early stages of its course.

We shall see this more clearly if we glance quickly through some of the outstanding events in human history.

We might begin at about 30,000 B.C.; for although remains of animals of our species are discovered in strata of much earlier date, yet it would appear that our kind emerged as manifestly successful over all competitors about thirty thousand years ago. If the date is a few thousand years wrong, the argument is unaffected.

For thousands of years following their emergence as "top animal", our ancestors lived as members of little wandering tribes, eating such animals, birds and fish as they could catch, and such berries, grains, fruits and nuts as they could find. In three important respects they had surpassed the apes and monkeys from whose great line they had diverged at some time and by some means that are not now precisely known. They had come to terms with fire; they regularly manufactured and used crude tools; and, as their caves still show, they had reached aesthetic potentialities which, in some directions, have not been surpassed even to the present day. Yet (to make a thoroughly Marxist judgment) their social and political organisation was conditioned by their economic means of getting their livelihood. Bluntly, they were scroungers; and for this reason they could not pass beyond the small and usually wandering tribe.

This went on until some ten thousand years ago when the first of our two genuinely epoch-making events began to make itself felt. This event was the discovery of agriculture. It did not happen suddenly all over the world. Thousands continued to live as scroungers long after millions had settled down as farmers. Nevertheless, by some such date as 7-6000 B.C. it was clear that man's developing future lay with the agricultural civilisations settled in the valleys of the Nile, Euphrates, Ganges and Yangtse, or with others of the same kind in other places. The essential fact was that agriculture gave to man the "magic" storable surplus over and above the needs of next week's living. Admittedly the vast majority of mankind still lived very close to the margin of starvation, either as slaves, serfs or peasants. This does not alter the fact that all civilisations, all kings and palaces, all priests and temples, all generals and great armies, all sculptors, architects, philosophers, playwrights, painters, musicians and scientists have been sustained on the thousands of little men at the bottom of the social pyramid who produced more food than they ate.

The many civilisations that reared themselves on this foundation differed fairly widely in organisation and ideology. But they almost all shared a number of important features in common. Almost, though not quite all were avowedly authoritarian in one way or another. All, by our present standards, were ignorant of the great nexus of laws of cause and effect which, even though we have not yet mastered them all, yet manifestly tie the whole physical world—indeed the whole universe—into some kind of self-consistent entity. In short, they were ignorant of Science. And finally, with marginal help from wind and water, they had to rely for their power on the muscles of men, women, children and animals. We may therefore describe these civilisations as constituting the authoritarian, pre-scientific and muscle-driven age of man.

This is the age which endured, with all its squalors and splendours, until "the day before yesterday". And enormous numbers of our fellow men and women—perhaps more than half of them—are still for all essential purposes living within that authoritarian, pre-scientific and muscle-driven age.

But we are not.

How far back in history need we go to discover the roots of change? We must certainly go as far as the middle of the eleventh century in western Europe; for it was within a few decades of our notorious 1066 that the most dynamic of our rugged ancestors diverted their energies from destructive marauding and settled down to a rough and rude but basically constructive way of life. Already they were building cathedrals; within 150 years they had established universities.

By the end of the fifteenth century we can clearly detect active minorities working within the old to create the new. We may take Columbus, Copernicus and Luther as symbolic of three important aspects of what was essentially a single complex change. They were about fifty, twenty-eight and eighteen years old in the first year of the sixteenth century.

Of the three, Columbus is probably the least important. He, and his ocean-going cannon-bearing ship, may be taken to represent that technological superiority which, from his day to August 1914, enabled the white western race to impose itself increasingly upon all the other races of man. *Sub specie aeternitatis* this event may not be decisively important; it happens to be significant to us because we live in the decades when all the other races are wrenching themselves free from our white western domination.

Luther has a much more long-term significance. Though he was himself authoritarian, yet his revolt may be taken to symbolise the whole of the egalitarian challenge to authority in all its forms. Copernicus, of course, symbolises all the subsequent discoveries of all the scientists, as well as the myriad clever devices which the technologists have superimposed on them.

Throughout the sixteenth century the coming change was still no more than latent; nothing had as yet emerged on such a scale as to demand the attention of large numbers of ordinary men and women. What date must we chose for the first public manifestation of the second of only two epoch-making events in human history?

Some people might put it as early as the second quarter of the seventeenth century when our own parliamentarians challenged in arms the divine right of kings; others might put it at the third quarter with the founding of the Royal Society. My own choice of date must fall into the third quarter of the eighteenth century.

Clive's victories in Bengal had made it certain that in due time white men would excercise a temporary dominance over the greater part of Asia and Africa. Wolfe's victory at Quebec had been less decisive; it had ensured only that the natives of North America would be driven from their wide hunting grounds by English-speaking and not by French-speaking Europeans.

The challenge to authority was about to express itself in the American Declaration of Independence; and the French Revolution lay only a few years further ahead. These lead on, as they were bound to do, to the challenge to the "divine right" of private property, of school-teachers and of parents in which we are involved right up to the present day.

But even more decisive, the two decades before and after 1760 saw, in Britain, the climacteric developments in textile machinery, in the smelting of iron ore with coke, and in rotary steam power.

We may, then, fairly take the third quarter of the eighteenth century as the point at which our western European ancestors first openly lead the human race out of the authoritarian, pre-scientific and muscle-driven age of man, and over the threshold of the egalitarian, science-minded, power-driven stage in human experience.

Questions asked at public discussions have shown that at this point there can be grave confusion about dates. Let us be as clear as we can: we have already considered three different dates according to the aspects of the process that engaged our attention. The deep roots, the first heavings of the vast energy that has driven the process ever since, were in the eleventh century; by the end of the fifteenth century we found active minorities consciously working towards the new; and we put the first unmistakable world-scale manifestation of the whole phenomenon into the second part of the eighteenth century.

But there is a fourth stage, and a much more recent date, that must now be considered.

Even those who might argue about my 1750-75, would agree that the whole process had well and truly burst through the surface of public events in our own country by the early decades of the nineteenth century. But it had not by any such date profoundly changed the deep feelings and basic thought-patterns of vast masses of our people. Active minorities, as we have seen, had been breaking away from the old ways of thinking and feeling for several centuries. But this does not mean that suddenly—say between 1775 and 1825—all the villagers of England were changed into modern-minded men, women and children. Very far from it. Deepest feelings and basic thought-patterns are absorbed from the whole atmosphere of our homes in the earliest years of our lives; and this atmosphere is largely created by our parents who, in their turn, had laid down their thought-patterns in their own homes some fifteen to twenty-five years before we were born.

Look, then, at a family whose ancestors moved into one of our growing textile towns in the late 1820s or early 1830s. Great-great-great grandfather (born 1800s) laid down his basic thinking habits in a village whose externals hardly differed in any essential from those of a village in the empire of Nebuchadnezzar. Only since great-great grandfather (born 1830s) has the family been exposed to any influence from technological apparatus and egalitarian discussion; and he is dead, as is great-grandad (born 1860s). Grand-father (born 1890s) may well be alive. Father (born 1920s) is hard at work; and his children may be worrying about the 11+.

Remembering how many families there must be among us whose ancestors moved even more recently into the egalitarian and technological environment, may it not very well be that it is only now—or at the most only in the last one or two generations—that we rather suddenly begin to meet in our Secondary Schools great "masses" of children who have effectively shaken off the characteristic and long-persisting feelings of the great epoch that is closing, so that their thought-patterns are now conditioned, far down into the depths, by the new age in which we have all so recently embarked? Putting it very crudely: As far as concerns anything that has importance for religious education, Christian missionaries are suddenly confronted with "a different kind of animal".

And this is a reminder that the vast change now in progress is evolutionary in its significance. Unlike the other great stages in evolution, there is now no significant change in the physiognomy of each separate creature. Judged by the standard test for specific difference, there can be no doubt that a posse of cave men and women, if brought here by time machine, could interbreed quite satisfactorily with our most eminent intellectuals. But does the test for critical evolutionary transformation now lie within the animal's body at all? True, each man is an animal; but is his animal nature the most significant thing about him? Surely his thoughts and his feelings about himself and about his relationship to the world around him are much more important. These are the things that mark him out as being a man. In this sense, then, the differences between *Being-a-Man* (*a*) in the age of the wandering scroungers, (*b*) in one of the historic agricultural civilisations, and (*c*) in our egalitarian science-minded and power-driven community, are at least as significant, evolution-wise, as were those between the fish and the amphibia, or between the reptiles and the mammals.

Using the word "creature" to include everything back to the hydrogen molecules, we are probably the first generation of creatures to take part in a great forward move in evolution *while dimly grasping the fact that we do so!*

If we do not press the analogy too far, it may sometimes be useful to think of the three distinct ages in man's history as the Babyhood, the Childhood and now the beginning of the Adolescence of the human race. It will be convenient, from time to time, to use these designations even if only for the sake of avoiding longer and clumsier phrases.

Using them, then, for this designatory purpose, it is true that the Church has enjoyed its long propaganda experience and won its wide propaganda success only within the Childhood of the human race. Today local success is sometimes won by a man in virtue of his outstanding Christian personality; but the Church, simply as such, has not yet shown that she can win propaganda success amongst the typical men, women and children who live in these early decades of the Adolescence of mankind.

This does not mean that anyone who shouts about a revolution of any kind is bound to be right; but it suggests that those who deny the need for any revolution in our teaching methods are very likely to be wrong.

And how does anyone feel about the whole prospect? Does he greet the need for a teaching revolution with a groan or with a cheer? This is immensely important because no one can effectively teach anything that makes him feel depressed. Probably in the last resort our attitude depends on whether we believe in religious progress. Put in this form, the question should not be dismissed lightly. All progress means movement; and movement of any kind must be movement from where we were before; those, then, who love the place where we were are bound to be hurt. This I have often found to be an absolutely decisive factor in the situation. Particularly when discussing the problem with small groups of ordained ministers I have found them just on the point of agreeing that something ought to be done, indeed that we ought to do it, until suddenly one of them slams the door on it by pointing out that if we did "*that*" somebody might be hurt. At all costs, we must not hurt anyone. And so, for fear of hurting a few score, we do not do the things for want of which thousands are dying a spiritual death.

But there may be deeper feelings about progress than these. In a sense "progress" is a dirty word. It was the battle-cry of our opponents. They were making progress when they broke free from the authoritarian religious superstitions; progress when they turned from things of the spirit to the ever-increasing technological production of things of the flesh; progress when they deserted the religion of Christ for the religion of Science. Around the turn of the last century, our grandparents over-optimistically supposed that this new religion would lead them to an earthly Utopia in a matter of decades. And what a disillusionment today!

This, surely, might be a point in our favour. There is a deep longing for progress of some kind. Might we not attract the children of this generation if we could suggest the possibility of religious progress—not perhaps dramatic in any decade, but relentless as the centuries unroll? Of course we must not cheat. We must not speak of religious progress if in fact there is no such thing. But if there is religious progress, then instead of sadly admitting that Christians do not now believe all that was believed a hundred years ago, why not joyously proclaim the religious advance?

When we look far back into the past, the progress is unmistakable. The expansion of the religious vision between the tribal God of Abraham and the universal personal God of the second Isaiah, forms the staple theme of much of our orthodox Old Testament teaching. It leads up to Christ.

But with Christ, it may be suggested, the development reaches its final climax, with no further change permissible. In one sense this can be true enough. Christ is the same yesterday, today and for ever. From God's side the Incarnation was His unique, complete and once-for-all initiative to which nothing can be added with the passing of the years. Does this mean that from man's side our appreciation and understanding of the Truth revealed in Jesus Christ must never change, never expand, never deepen or grow? Is this historically true? In point of fact, has there been change and expansion since earliest Christian times, or not?

Only quite recently I was astonished to learn from Leslie Weatherhead in his book *A Plain Man looks at the Cross*, that for nine hundred years the Christian Church was held in thrall to a theory which explained the Atonement in terms of Christ's Death and Passion being "the ransom-price paid by God to the Devil, so that the latter, who had men in his clutches, would let them go and allow them to escape the pains of hell."[1] This theory, he says, was put forward by Irenaeus in the second century, believed by Gregory of Nyssa (221-96) and by Augustine (354-430), and held sway until displaced by the "satisfaction" theory offered by Anslem (1033-1109).

Let it be said that this strange notion at least enabled some thirty generations of barbarians to catch a fleeting glimpse of the extent of God's love that would pay such a price to save men from such a fate. But are Christians bound to believe such rubbish for ever? Where, anyway, can we now find any trace of it, except perhaps in the assumptions underlying some of the verses in some of the hymns that are still sung in some of our Secondary Schools to the mystification of some of the pupils.[2]

And in relatively more recent times, was it religious progress when the Bible was made available to all who could read their native tongue? Was it religious progress when men began to understand that at the Eucharist, the miracle was the coming of the Essence and Life of Christ in the mind and heart of the faithful communicant, and not in an external and physical transformation of bread into flesh? Was it religious progress

[1] *Op. cit.* (Wyvern Books), p. 60.

[2] See verse three in the hymn that begins "Ye choirs of new Jerusalem", *Hymns Ancient and Modern*, No: 125.

when we freed ourselves from the hideous doctrine of Predestination—except, of course, in some of the Thirty-nine Articles to which every vicar is invited to swear with his tongue in his cheek.[1]

"The Lord hath yet more light and truth to break forth from his word." So sang the Pilgrim Fathers and it is just as true today as it was then. And we must use every means to "beat down Satan under our feet", and enable the children of this generation to know that in religion, as in science, the whole human race is learning all the time. One of the most moving passages I have ever read in any contemporary writing is in Professor Whitehead's *Science and the Modern World*: I have quoted it many times before:

> "Religion emerged into human experience mixed with the crudest fancies of barbaric imagination. Gradually, slowly, steadily, the vision recurs in history under nobler form and with clearer expression. It is the one element in human experience which persistently shows an upward trend. It fades, and then recurs. But when it renews its force, it recurs with added richness and purity of content. The fact of the religious vision, and its history of persistent expansion, is our one ground for optimism. Apart from it, human life is a flash of occasional enjoyment lighting up a mass of pain and misery, a bagatelle of transient experience."[2]

I have only once read contemporary sentences which moved me more than those words of Whitehead's. I read them nearly a quarter of a century ago in W. R. Maltby's *Significance of Jesus*.

> "There is, I believe, already within our reach, a nobler, more reasonable, more comprehensive message than ever our fathers knew—and this not because we are wiser, or even more sincere than they, but because it is not for nothing that the Spirit of God has been at work upon the minds of men during these years of amazing research and fearless interrogation. That better message, however, has not yet been so articulated as to

[1] For a recent protest against this example of contemporary Church cowardice, see *The Thirty-nine Articles*, by Dr. W. R. Matthews, Dean of St. Paul's (Hodder and Stoughton).

[2] *Op. cit.* (C.U.P.), p. 238.

reach the average man, and if he asks only where and how to begin, he may have to wait long before he hears any satisfying answer."[1]

And where has the amazing research gone on? Where has the fearless interrogation gone forward? It has gone on through the physicists' microscopes, in the chemists' test-tubes, under the archaeologists' hammers and in the studies of the penetrating textual critics. The work of these men, far from stirring our resentment and leaving us depressed because of its corrosive effect on the old ways of teaching, should rouse our enthusiasm as that without which the nobler message would never have come within our tenuous reach.

The religious vision fades, says Whitehead. And who can deny that it has faded in the course of recent centuries? It is due, then, to "recur with added richness and purity of content". This is not defeat or retreat. This is advance!

And consider Maltby's "average man" living so often today with a "God-shaped blank in his heart", because he can no longer respond to the old presentation of Christian truth; and because the nobler, more reasonable, more comprehensive message is not yet being articulated, either in classrooms or from pulpits, in a form that can reach him.

The necessary revolution to which we are called, is not something to feel depressed about. On the contrary, it is the most thrilling challenge that anyone could meet.

The rest of the book, then, is an exploration to discover, if possible, the general direction, or some of the directions, in which we may have to move if the revolution is to be made. It is not, as it were, an "A.A. Route Map" showing every detailed twist and turn of the road that will lead us from where we are to the revolution's final consumation. Indeed we never find out "exactly" how to make revolutions by sitting down and thinking out every detail in advance; we find out how to make revolutions by making them. That is to say, in this case, that we shall start to hack out the actual road and to find our way in detail around particular obstacles when a fairly large number of teachers, in classrooms and in pulpits, perceive the need and

[1] *Op. cit.* (S.C.M.), p. 39 of original edition.

experimentally set off in the indicated direction so as to see what happens. It is particularly important that this should be borne in mind by critics who feel themselves emotionally predisposed against admitting the need for any revolution of any kind; as otherwise they will feel confident that they can urge other people to deny the general need simply because one particular author speaks of revolution without having demonstrated exactly how we shall circumvent every one of the many obstacles which the critic perceives in the path that lies ahead.

CHAPTER THREE

CLASSROOM DETAILS

THERE ARE ONE or two almost technical classroom questions that are bound to come up sooner or later; and it might be as well to get them out of the way now, because otherwise it may seem to many teachers that much of what follows has to be condemned as impracticable when considered against the kind of atmosphere that normally prevails in the R.E. period as they know it—an atmosphere that is often unpropitious towards serious learning, to say the least.

One day, during a long walk into London at Easter in 1961, I passed the time by dropping into step with groups of teenagers who were going my way so as to ask them about this atmosphere in the R.E. lessons at their schools, or at the schools from which they had recently escaped. The resulting conversations did not lend themselves to statistical analysis. Nor was the verdict unanimous. I recall one particular pair who were enthusiastic about the vigour and open-minded intelligence of a young man who had recently come to take charge of their religious instruction. But it will be no surprise to most teachers to know that at the end of the day my general impression was that these young people came from schools where the R.E. period is despised. It comes round once a week while mathematics and English come round every day. A surprisingly large number of pupils know that it is required by law to find its place, just once, in each week's programme; and many suspect that this is the only reason why it is included at all. Except in the rarest instances, it leads to no examination result. In short, it does not matter. There is no need to bother about it or to take it seriously; no one in the school ever has; it is the school tradition not to do so. On the contrary, it is the period in which, by long established custom, we muck about, and see how much we can get away with.

What chance has a teacher of arousing new interest by trying a new line if his class meets him in this kind of mood? Unless he does something rather special in the very moment of his encounter with his new charges when he comes face to face with them in the middle of September, he may lose the battle for the whole year in his fight to keep order for the first three-quarters of an hour. Somehow or other the usual atmosphere must be dispelled, at once, by a blast of personal fresh air.

My suggestion, then, to any teacher who finds himself invited to take an R.E. period, at any rate with any form between second and sixth in any Secondary School, is that he should ask the head teacher three questions:

"May I be sure of your backing in the unlikely event that some inquiry shows that I am following the Agreed Syllabus in the spirit rather than in the letter?"

"May I change the title of the period on the timetable, from 'Religious Education' to 'Religion and Life Discussion Period'?"

"*May I have two periods per week?*"

The need for the first of these questions is adequately covered by half a dozen sentences from the Sheffield report that has already been referred to:

> "Whilst it is true," say the authors, "that many Agreed Syllabuses have been revised at least once, the fact remains that the feeling of any teacher confronted for the first time with an Agreed Syllabus must be one of despair. . . . It takes a well-trained person to affirm that a syllabus is too cumbersome, that the work cannot be completed in the time available, and that it is necessary to make a judicious selection of material. In fairness it must be said that those who have compiled the Agreed Syllabuses usually explain in the introduction that their proposals are to be taken as a basis for such selection. It appears, however, that in a considerable proportion of secondary schools this latitude is not accepted. There is no doubt that to most non-specialists the Agreed Syllabus remains . . . a burden with which they cannot cope. The results of this wrong approach to the problem of the

content of the religious knowledge lesson are disastrous."[1]

The need for two periods has already been tentatively suggested. The statutory minimum is a formal insult. How can any assistant teacher be expected to convey the impression that religion really matters, when the head teacher has proclaimed in the timetable that it matters half as much as physics, one third as much as P.E., one-quarter as much as geography and one-fifth as much as maths? Of course a teacher may not find himself invited to take R.E. until after the head has drawn up the year's programme; and if the proposed R.E. period is the only one when the teacher will meet the form in question, then it may be no more than basic truth when he is told that with the best will in the world it is too late to start playing ducks and drakes with a piece of work that has eaten up two or three weeks of the head's summer holiday. But if the teacher has other periods with the same form, no administrative difficulty arises.

"Sir, I could give up my Tuesday afternoon maths to it."

"Ah, yes, Mr. Sidgwick, so you could; but . . . h'm . . . well, ah. . . . I don't quite like the sound of that; after all, maths. . . ."

With any such reply, the teacher ought to refuse to take the single insulting R.E. period. But . . . well, yes, I know . . . sometimes we have to give up the ideal principles, for the sake of a quiet life. Or do we?

The point about changing the title to "Religion and Life Discussion Period" will be granted at once, I believe, by the minority of teachers who are already making a success of their R.E. periods. The need for it is spelled out very clearly in *Teenage Religion*, the recently published report of a research group appointed by the Institute of Christian Education under the chairmanship of Harold Loukes. This report is compulsory reading for anyone concerned in any way with religious teaching. For the sake of those who have not yet met it, it must suffice to say here that the first part is a set of edited scripts from tape recordings taken "live" in a number of secondary classrooms; the second part is an analysis, with copious quotations, from written comments made by over five hundred

[1] *Religious Education in Secondary Schools* (Nelson), p. 47.

pupils on some of the most outstanding passages taken from the tapes. The last part contains the conclusions and suggestions of the group. Of these, it would be fair to say that the most outstanding and confident can be summed up in the one word; "Discuss!" It would be pointless here to reargue the case that Loukes makes so unanswerably; a single quotation from one of the children's comments must serve:

> "Before last year I began to think of R.I. Lessons as uninteresting; we were told things out of the Bible and we just had to accept them as true. (It was hard luck if we had our doubts.) But now we've reached our fourth year we can discuss, and I am sure when I say that I am not the only one, who now looks forward to them."

Assuming, then, that the head agrees to all the teacher's requests, he can meet his class in September with "Now that you have come up from form two (or as the case may be) we shall throw over the usual kind of teaching; and in these periods, twice a week, we shall have discussions about Life." He will do well to tell the class from the start that in the first period each week, he will usually decide the subject for discussion himself and may "take the floor" for an opening lead of five, ten or even fifteen minutes before throwing the subject open to the class. In each second weekly period the class will be free to discuss any subject under the sun with nothing barred. This will involve choosing a form captain (if none is chosen already) and a small committee, to receive suggested subjects from all members of the class and to pick pupils a week in advance to give the opening lead on next week's chosen subject.

If teacher and class do not spontaneously find all the themes they need, there are first-class detailed suggestions in *Teenage Religion*: and S.C.M. have produced some excellent little discussion sheets, called *Talk About*, which give quite probable real life situations in which some young man or woman is faced with moral choice. Their wall posters called *Focus* are also valuable.

My only anxiety about these discussion sheets, as also about

Teenage Religion, is their implication that the whole difficulty lies in raising the questions. Harold Loukes divides his practical suggestions for classroom procedure into four parts of which the third is *The Christian Interpretation*; and of this stage he says that it

> "represents familiar teaching material with no unusual demand except, perhaps, a greater readiness to listen to argument about it than teachers could expect if they were teaching trigonometry."

This seems to imply that once the children have been led to ask the religious questions vividly and in a contemporary setting, then the average teacher will know well enough how to hand out the twentieth-century answers. Surely a very doubtful proposition! At any rate I am writing this book in order to test it. And meanwhile I can only hope that what has been said already will assure any practising teacher that it ought not to be impossible, at the start of a term's work with a secondary form, to lift the whole programme out of the non-co-operative atmosphere that now bedevils so many of our religious teaching periods.

CHAPTER FOUR

WHAT WILL NOT BE CHANGED

REMEMBERING, THEN, THAT our purpose in creating a co-operative atmosphere in the classroom is to start work on a revolution, let us first consider how much there is that will not have to be changed. Briefly and comprehensively, *we are not considering a new religion.* This has to be stated explicitly; since experience in public discussions has shown that otherwise the whole argument may be rejected by people who wrongly suppose it far more iconoclastic than it really is.

To particularise, there is to be no change of attitude to the Church. This may not be apparent because the book is undeniably a criticism of the methods adopted by Christian teachers with approval—or at least without vocal disapproval—from the present leaders of the Church. And I have already displayed my indignation against all Christian teachers, lay and ordained, for allowing the disastrous ignorance of the overwhelming majority of the children who answered my question about Jonah.

But there is something more important than the particular company of bishops, clergy and school-teachers who may or may not have been at fault in having used, too long, the teaching methods appropriate to olden days. There is the whole Church Militant here on Earth—the mystical body of the Lord—the persistent living witness to His Truth yesterday, today and for all time. If I now tried to compose something new about the Church it might seem rather like a feeble attempt to put a little sugar on pills that follow in later chapters. It seems much better to quote a few paragraphs that I wrote some fifteen years ago. For indeed, many who sneer at the Church from outside and point to the undeniable follies and crimes perpetrated by its leaders both in distant times and now, often have no conception of the hideous forces that are unleashed just as soon as a noble cause is enshrined—or rather encased —in an organisation.

Our critics, I wrote in 1947, sometimes talk as if we could somehow carry on without a Church of any sort or kind. They tell us that "we could easily believe in the simple teaching of Jesus if only it wasn't for the Church."

But could we? Could we really do without any organisation at all?

Organisation is a curious thing. People who take part in organisation find themselves exposed to dangers and temptations that are in many ways more powerful and subtle than those which are met in unorganised or so-called private life. And yet organisation seems necessary.

In this world of ours, evil can often do fairly well without any particular organisation. We do not need a Royal Society for the Promotion of Slums. Slums come into being of their own accord. It is quite otherwise with good.

For a good cause to prosper, it is not usually enough that someone should have a good idea, or even that a lot of people should agree that his idea is good. Very little actually happens until a number of people come together and take hold of the good idea and drive it through by their organised mental effort and their organised physical sweat.

What is true of all good causes may be equally true of the cause of Good itself. Will men effectively hunger and thirst after righteousness if no one ever organises the business of telling them about it? Is it supposed that "natural" goodness, left to itself, will make headway against natural apathy, natural ignorance, natural self-centredness and downright natural evil?

"Thou shalt love thy neighbour as thyself." "As you would that others should do unto you, do you also unto them." "Inasmuch as you did it to the least of these My brethren, you did it unto Me."

This is the simple teaching of Jesus.

Certainly we all dishonour these sentences in our lives. But we know them; they are part of the very atmosphere we breathe;

even when other and (would you say?) more natural influences succeed in pulling us in other directions, these words of Jesus exercise their subtle magnetism upon us and upon the whole environment.

Now there must be, and indeed there are, many passages in the writings of such men as Plato and Marcus Aurelius quite as worthy of remark as these sentences from the New Testament. A few resolute scholars know the words of these philosophers because they find them in books on the less-used shelves of our libraries. But the rest of us—the miners and the mothers, the typists and the chemists, the production managers, engine drivers and members of parliament—we do not know what Plato or Aurelius wrote. And yet we know the very words of Jesus.

Why?

Because the Spirit of Jesus has inspired men and women to start from tiny beginnings and to build up a massive organisation; and then, despite all the temptations and all the failures and all the crimes, to sustain it down to this day.

Believe in the simple teaching of Jesus if it were not for the Church . . . ?

On the contrary; if it were not for the Church we should hardly even hear of Him, let alone believe in His teaching.[1]

In any case the teacher who is trying to make a success of his Religion and Life Discussion Periods unconditionally must go to church. If he never, or hardly ever, goes to any church or chapel, the children will soon know all about it; and he will be "saying" to them more clearly than in any words: "This, which I tell you is more important than all else, is not worth forty-five minutes a week." If a teacher says that he cannot get through the term unless Sunday is a long lie-in followed by total relaxation, then in all towns and many country parishes he will find regular services on a weekday at such times as will allow him to reach school at 8.45.

[1] *Nothing Left to Believe?* (Longmans), p. 5.

And I add one further point because of the shameful fact of having forgotten it until reminded by another a year or so ago. The teacher should pray for the children. Or if the word sounds too stark to the many teachers who in fact take R.E. despite their genuine difficulty in believing in the transcendent Godhead Who "hears our prayers", then let it be put another way. At some time before each lesson the teacher should withdraw himself from the racket of the school timetable, even if only for ten minutes, so as to reach down, through his own Inner Light, and deliberately hold up the children, in imagination, to the whole stream of eternal Love and Truth.

We ought particularly to consider those who left Christianity, probably during their teens, and have now come back to it. They were often driven out precisely because the Church was offering childish dogma to their adolescent minds. Then, in their own way, and very often through some mystical experience given to them by the Holy Spirit, they came back to Christian belief—but no longer at the childish level. In many cases they came back to Christianity, but not to the Church.

This is wrong! A. W. Watts writes of the doctrines, holy books and creeds that can become millstones if we suppose that we may possess God within them, and continues:

> "In the past it has often happened that souls who recognised this left the fellowship of the Church and ceased altogether from the sacramental life. This, however, is still an adolescent procedure. . . . The true mystic discovers in these forms altogether new depths of meaning. *Only sheer spiritual pride could stop him from worshipping at an altar with souls lacking his own insight.*"[1]

Fortunately we have in Holy Communion a service that can appeal to the hearts of those who still live with "the devout faith" of a bygone age, and can reveal layer after layer of meaning to those who are strained forward to the "baptised science of the future". As this is the first time that I have taken phrases from Frederick Stokes, I cannot pass by without calling

[1] *Behold the Spirit* (John Murray), p. 97 (my italics).

attention to his breath-taking prophecy written as long as three-quarters of a century ago. It is printed next after the title page of this book.

Good luck, then, to all who are experimenting with all kinds of new forms of ritual. A large part of our religious future rests in their keeping. But they would agree, I think, with the whole spirit of this book in that they are not looking for something absolutely new; but for new ways of handling the same basic Truth and the same Service as we have already.

More immediately important for the main argument that we have in hand, is the fact that there needs to be no basic change in the religious teaching that goes on in Primary Schools and Sunday Schools.

In passing it may be said that in these days, when increasing numbers of children go to modern-built and modern-run Primary Schools, it simply will not do to collect them into the dingy old rooms with the tattered old pictures where Sunday Schools were so often conducted in olden days. Teaching, in such surroundings, does not merely do no good; it does harm by stamping it into the children's hearts that religion is dingy and tattered. This may be one of the reasons why some of our liveliest priests seem to have a bias against Sunday Schools as such. I think they are wrong. But they are only wrong in relation to those Sunday Schools to which someone is giving enormously more up-to-date attention and far more downright hard work that was normally given to the "average" Sunday School a generation or two ago.

But this is superficial. The essential is that what the Primary School and Sunday School are trying to do is basically right. True enough that their teaching, particularly in the last couple of years, could often be given in detail a more contemporary emphasis and interpretation. For example, since just over a year ago I have been taking, as a Bible Class, four boys who came up to me as twelve-year-olds from a first-rate village Primary School and a very creative Sunday School. They had no hesitation or difficulty in telling me, in their own words, that there is no historic truth in the first few chapters of Genesis and that these early stories have value for us now as allegorical expression of eternal truth about man and God. I mention this fact because, contrary to what is often said by many, it is simply untrue to suppose that young and tender faith is destroyed by early exposure to modern Christian knowledge.

The important point, however, is that it is right, at primary school age, to put before the children the wonder stories of the Bible—New Testament and Old—so as to allow the "magic" to do its work in their pre-scientific hearts. Let them take it straight; let us not interfere if they are "seeing" God as a Big Man who watches and loves them from the sky; let them learn it and set it out in the sand tray and write it and draw it and model it and mime it and act it to the top of their bent. This is all absolutely right.

At this point in the argument there will be no difficulty in carrying with me the average parson and the average parson's wife. It is the modern-minded school-teacher who will need persuading. And persuasion, odd as it may seem, comes from evolution.

It is well known that during the nine months between conception and birth we "recapitulate" all the main stages in the evolutionary tree. That is to say, we live as amoeba, as little fish, as little amphibia, as little mammals, as little monkeys, before coming into the world as little people. Now it has just been suggested that evolution has not stopped. There are no longer any specific changes in the individual animal; but the change from the authoritarian pre-scientific muscle-driven age that lies behind us to the egalitarian, science-minded power-driven age that lies ahead, is a change evolutionary in its significance. If this is so, it necessarily follows that even though the human animal is in a sense fully evolved at birth, yet the human spirit now has another evolutionary stage to recapitulate on the way to living as an adult human individual within what I would describe as still an adolescent human society. He has to recapitulate—that is to say he has to live through as personal experience—the simple unquestioning childlike faith which served, all through adult life, for the vast mass of his ancestors from far distant times right down until a very few generations before his own birth. He cannot rest in this childlike faith all his life as most of his ancestors could; and this not because he is better or worse than they, but because he lives in a society which has only very recently moved into the adolescent stage wherein all kinds of questions will ask themselves and cannot be answered within the old formulae.

But, though he cannot rest all his life in the childlike stage, he must, evolution-wise, live through it. If, because of parental ignorance or neglect, or sometimes because of misguided parental love and open-mindedness, he does not live through the experience of this stage while he is still too innocent to ask our modern questions, it is difficult to know how the loss will ever be made good to him . . . except that "with God all things are possible". This is, indeed, the most obvious meaning of the saying of Jesus: "Except you receive the Kingdom of God as a little child, you shall in no wise enter therein." We shall come to another, and, as some may think, a profounder meaning in the same saying at a later stage.

In all the rest of this book we shall be considering the problems of religious teaching during the years when the child begins to move into adolescence—years when all the problems and questions of individual maturity within our modern world will begin to loom ahead.

It will be assumed that the adolescents we are talking about will have had some kind of experience—not, perhaps, as full and vigorous as it ought to have been, but at any rate some experience—of the childlike stage of spiritual evolution. The assumption is a fair one, not only because they will have passed through Primary Schools where the wonder stories of the Bible will have been put before them. If this were all, it might be answered that any good effect of schooling would be more than cancelled by the bad effect of homes in many of which the child sees no sign of religious belief from one week's end to the next—and this at all social and economic levels in our society. Doubtless a few more generations of this kind of home life would destroy even the best work that the primary school teachers could do. But our case is not yet quite so bad as that. After all, we are affected for good as well as for ill by what lies in the subconscious; and the forces of racial memory—even those handed down from fairly recent generations—are likely to be fairly strong. Therefore, though a child's parents may seldom or never do anything that outwardly suggests their smallest concern for religion, yet he and they still live fairly close to the generations when the childlike faith could be believed, and was in fact believed by millions, in all its simple childlike form.

As we work, we need not suppose that the children have a complete spiritual vacuum under their feet. Underneath all the questions and doubts and worries of this age, the simple faith is there. It ought not to be an impossible task to offer the basic Christian truths in terms that are acceptable in the egalitarian, science-minded power-driven age to which the whole human race is now advancing.

This brings us to the most daunting question in this chapter—indeed in the whole book. What is the basic Christian truth that we hope the children will learn? What is it that Christians believe?

> "I believe in one God the Father Almighty, Maker of heaven and earth, and of all things visible and invisible:
>
> "And in one Lord Jesus Christ, the only-begotten Son of God. . . . Who for us men and for our salvation came down from heaven. . . . And was crucified also for us under Pontius Pilate. . . . And the third day he rose again. . . . And sitteth on the right hand of the Father. . . .
>
> "And I believe in the Holy Ghost, the Lord and Giver of Life. . . . And I look for the Resurrection of the dead, And the life of the world to come."

These splendid words, and many many others of the same tone and quality have conveyed an intimation of the Truth to millions of human souls during the greater part of the last two thousand years; to most they have conveyed this Truth dimly and only occasionally; to a few, vividly and almost all the time. The only difficulty about these words, and about all the others that have the same venerable overtones, is that thousands of men, women and children of the present day may hear them or read them and can then in all sincerity ask of them: "Yes, but what on earth do they really mean to my life here and now?" It follows from this that some people enthusiastically accept them with their lips while having almost no feeling for real religion in their lives, others consciously reject the words out of hand despite the fact that in a very real sense they are living their lives religiously; and yet others (far more numerous than either of these, and far more disastrous in their ultimate significance) can say with an apparent show of superficial truth that in these days it really does not seem to make much difference one way or the other whether anyone says he believes in Christianity or not.

This is a serious thing to hear said, even though it does not cover the whole of the truth. For most of us must know of individual Christians here and there whose Christian faith is shining out of them with such force as to make them quite different in kind from the general run of people whom we meet. Nevertheless, it is difficult to persuade people that the Christian truth is more important than anything else in life if many of our hearers, having divided their acquaintances into those who do and those who do not say they believe it, tell us quite sincerely that they cannot detect any clear difference between them.

So it becomes necessary to try to offer the basic Christian truth in different language. And yet the effort cannot be made without at least attempting to disarm criticism in advance by proclaiming the impossiblity of the task in words used by Hilary who was bishop of Poitiers in the fourth century:

> "Alas, we are driven by the faults of our heretical opponents to do things unlawful, to scale heights inaccessible . . . to strain our weak human language in the utterance of things beyond its scope. . . . Hence, what should be matter for silent religious meditation must now needs be imperilled by exposure in words."[1]

[1] From *De Trinitate*, quoted from *Reason and Revelation*, by J. R. Illingworth (Macmillan), p. 128.

It gives me an immense thrill to remember that these words were written more than sixteen hundred years ago; and that they have stood ever since as warning that no words ever express the whole Truth, and as further warning that no verbal formula is ever sacrosanct. With these warnings in mind, let us do what we may to express the unchanging Truth in meaningful twentieth-century phrases:

> "Everything that happens is, and always has been and always will be linked together into a living Whole. All the apparently separate particulars that go to make up this Whole are held together and sustained (and always have been held together and sustained) by conscious Will and Purpose whose ways are those of creative self-giving suffering Love. Most created particulars (stones, acorns, cows) seem to exist and to live in accordance with the divine Will whether they want to or not. But with men it is otherwise. The old words were that 'God created man in His own image'. Today we had better say that each human being, though far from omnipotently free, yet enjoys a certain measure of freedom and may either try to understand the divine Purpose and expose himself to be found by the divine Will so as to show forth some part of the self-giving Love; or he may pursue some other aim, or no aim at all. And the ultimate Worth of each man's life depends upon the extent of his alignment with the eternal Purpose."

Some of what I have just written would be rejected, I fear, by some religious men, particularly perhaps by Hindus and Buddhists; although, with the necessary interpretations, even they would accept a good deal of it. Almost all of it would be accepted by followers of all the religions which spring up from the blunt assertion: "We believe in God". I think it would be difficult to find many Christians who would condemn any of it as outrageously wrong or grossly misleading.

But all Christians would go far beyond any of the words that I have so far used in the claims that we would make for Jesus Christ. And we would say of these claims that they are not trivial or optional, but crucial and essential to the real acceptance and understanding of all the rest. For nearly twenty centuries these claims have been enshrined in the words:

> God gave His only Son Jesus Christ to suffer death for our redemption.

I will try to rephrase them:

> The conscious Will and Purpose behind all Life took a *unique* initiative, and with the intent of displaying the very nature of the Will and Purpose, made a *unique* incursion into the visible, tangible, humdrum world of men and women, in and through the life and teaching and crucifixion of Jesus of Nazareth. His Spirit is alive and active in the world today, and is available to all who humbly seek Him.

When I said just now that no Christian would condemn my language as grossly misleading, I did not mean that none would criticise in detail. On the contrary, there is no seriously-thinking Christian who would not at some point want to cross out some of my words and put in others which would express Truth more nearly. I have spelled it all out in this crude, lame language at this stage so that it may be seen that there is not here, or in any other part of the book, any attempt to water down anything in the essential Christian message, or to substitute some entirely new doctrine for anything that has formed part of the *kerygma* since the days of the earliest Apostles. The words that I have used make an honest attempt "to scale heights inaccessible and to strain our weak human language in the utterance of what should be matter for silent religious meditation." The Truth which they inadequately portray is the same Truth that Christians have tried to proclaim for just over seven hundred thousand days.

The words evoke images in the minds of those who hear them; and I have chosen them because I believe that today they evoke images that correspond reasonably well with the deeper, fuller apprehension of the same Truth that has been given to the saints of Christian history and is given to Christian saints today.

And what a staggering Truth it is! And, in these days, how appallingly difficult genuinely and whole-heartedly to believe it.

The very fact of this great difficulty gives us a clue to the *malaise* which must afflict many of our teachers who have conscientiously undertaken, say, a couple of R.E. periods within each week's teaching programme; and it might be as well to draw the source of it into the open so as to take a good look at it. As I see it, our people, and particularly those of them between the ages of twelve and fifty, are divided into a majority for whom (if they ever think about it seriously at all) a genuine belief in the Christian faith is very difficult; and a minority for whom it is very much easier. Now *a priori* considerations suggest what personal observation confirms, namely, that far more than half of our ordained clergy and ministers, and rather more than half of the R.E. specialists in our schools, are drawn from the minority who find Christian faith quite easy. How difficult for them, then, deeply to sympathise with the majority whom they are trying to help.

To take a single example: How often, I wonder, have I heard a preacher in the pulpit contending against those of us who say that the Christian beliefs are incredible; "but," says he, as if everyone ought to be overwhelmed by what is coming next,

> "if anyone had told your grandparents that a horse could run a race in Kentucky with the victory witnessed, in the very moment of its winning, by ladies and gentlemen sitting in their parlours in Balham and in Ez-sur-Mer; why, those ancestors of yours would have condemned it as absolutely incredible. And yet it has come to pass. Why, then, should you find it incredible when Christians speak of God?"

If one did not know that it was offered innocently, one would condemn the argument as a downright insult to our intelligence. Cannot the preachers understand what happens when all sorts of alleged "wonders" authenticate themselves to us just as soon as they can be tracked back to identifiable machines—visible and cunning assemblages built up out of pieces of metal, glass and plastic—all obeying "the laws of nature" and producing their results by processes which most of us will never come within ten years of understanding; but, as we all know perfectly well, by processes understood by the teams of backroom boffins as clearly as we understand the principles of the dear old steam engines that are just about passing out of use? Cannot the preachers understand that most of the people who have been rubbing shoulders for the last two or three generations with "wonders" of this kind, find it fantastically difficult to believe in a conscious loving Will and Purpose Which—or Who—cannot be specifically tracked back to any identifiable assemblage of twirling electrons, neutrons and protons; but is said to be immanent in and transcendent above the totality of all things?

What I am trying to say is that the teacher with his couple of R.E. periods per week almost certainly belongs to the majority who find faith difficult. He suffers an indefinable "something" because he feels that in these R.E. periods he ought to follow, as closely as he can, the methods adopted by the experts—the ordained ministers and the R.E. specialists. But these, for the most part, are men and women who find faith easy! I am suggesting, therefore, to the "average teacher" that the way out of his *malaise* is to stop feeling unhappy and perhaps rather guilty about not liking the ways of minority experts; and to look around for ways that better fit his own deep feelings and basic thought patterns . . . and those of the majority of his pupils.

There is one other truth that must be mentioned before we end a chapter dealing with all that will not be changed in the course of our impending revolution in teaching methods. Indeed in this case it is rather too little to say that it will not be changed. It will have to be taken down from the level of high theological discussion where it is already widely recognised, and applied at secondary school level.

This theological Truth has been particularly associated in recent times with the work of Dr. Karl Barth. He tells us—to put it simply—that the Truth of God is not, and cannot be, passed around horizontally "in penny packets" from man to man; but strikes down vertically, by the grace of the Holy Spirit, to man from God.

Now I am bound to say that I should find difficulty in describing exactly how this truth applied to the many millions of "barbarians" who seem to have been converted to some kind of Christian faith on the authoritative proclamation of many missionaries at many times and places during the authoritarian pre-scientific and muscle-driven age of man. But I am more and more convinced that we are in desperate need of understanding this truth, and of learning how to apply it, in action, in the classroom situation of today. To do this, we may have to rid ourselves of some of our teaching arrogance; for it is arrogance when a human teacher supposes that his words, his argument, his up-to-date illustrations and his marshalling of Bible texts will carry the Truth of God just as if it were the same kind of thing as the truth of Pythagoras. It needs a trace of humility to understand that in religious teaching, the teacher's part may be to remove obstacles that stand in the way, and to dispose the hearts and minds of adolescents favourable towards the reception of the Truth of God; and after that, to stand clear and leave the rest to the Holy Spirit.

Nor is it any use for the teacher to complain that he never says anything to lead the class to suppose that they will find the truth of God in his words and arguments. It is always to be remembered that situations "speak".

They speak far louder than casual words; they even speak a good deal louder than sentences which are slowly and deliberately enunciated with all possible verbal emphasis . . . unless these sentences are backed up by a whole course of action which is wholly consistent with what has been said. Failing such action, the situation shouts down the earnest verbiage.

Then take the situation that we are thinking about: the teacher, the blackboard and some thirty or forty children sitting at their little desks. This situation "says" in the clearest possible language: "Sit up, listen, do what I say, make an effort, and *you* will get your *maths* from *me*." And it works. It is true. If they sit up and listen and do what he says and make an effort they will in fact get their maths—(at any rate in many perfectly proper meanings of the phrase)—"from him".

And then the bell goes; and in comes the R.E. teacher. Apart from that, the situation is just the same. Whatever the R.E. teacher may say, the situation is saying: "Sit up, listen, do what I say, make an effort, and *you* will get *belief in God* from *me*."

It is possible that this will not do very much harm to rather dim children. Some of them may be living with their basic thought-patterns still more closely attuned to the bygone age than to the present. Perhaps some of these will actually get belief in God from teacher's lesson. But what of the children with greater intelligence or vitality? What about those whose minds are more and more deeply affected by the age in which we now begin to live? Are we not directing them towards probable spiritual disaster? Indeed, the greater their all-round alertness, the greater their seriousness and integrity, the greater will be the risk.

They are being offered, in effect, "teacher's penny packet"; and if theologically accepted truths are to be applied to practical situations at all, the one certainty is that they will not find God inside it. God is not passed around horizontally from teacher to child. Maybe that in many cases, while the child is still sheltered in the atmosphere of a good school, no ill-effect will break through into consciousness. But what happens when he goes into the outside world and meets its characteristic doubts and challenges? We are asking for superhuman insight from the teenager if we believe that he then will say: "I was wrong in supposing that I should learn my faith in God from anything handed out to me by teacher. I must now therefore hold my Whole Being alertly open to the possibility of one day receiving the truth of God from the one true Source." How much more likely that he will say: "That's religion—that was." Statistics about church attendance during the later years of adolescence suggest that something of this kind is what actually happens.

We are looking, then, not for some new verbal formula, but for a course of action—a new approach to the teaching problem

—which will prevent the classroom situation from tramlining the children into this kind of disaster. In the hope of finding it, we must look more closely at the basic thought-patterns that were typical of an age that has ended, and at the changes that are being brought about by the age that has just begun.

CHAPTER FIVE

OLD WAYS OF THOUGHT

THIS BUSINESS OF people's thought-patterns at other times is a difficult one. We are not simply considering the things they had to think about; if we were, we could form a pretty good idea by looking at pictures by contemporary painters. We are not even considering individual thoughts; for we can, with rather greater difficulty, form some idea of these by reading books and pamphlets written at the time. Underneath the things that are thought about and underneath the individual thoughts, are the basic thought-patterns within and along which the whole of the thinking process is conducted. The basic thought-patterns sustain the whole array of individual thoughts much as the skeleton sustains the array of muscle, fat, skin and clothes that we recognise when we meet each other in the streets. But we seldom remember skeletons. Indeed I have once or twice caught whole audiences by telling them there are a couple of skeletons on the platform. They readily follow me about as I look under the tablecloth, behind the rostrum and out into the wings until I remind them that one is in me and the other in the chairman.

Similarly we often attend to our individual thoughts, but we seldom notice our basic thought-patterns. We simply take them for granted and do not usually even remember that we have them. It is no easy matter honestly to appreciate that in other days there were whole generations of men, women and children whose thought-patterns were quite different from our own. But there were; and the effort must be made.

The difference has been partly, though not wholly, indicated within the rough and ready title that we have so often given to the age from which we are emerging.

We called it authoritarian. True, it was not always so; there were exceptions, particularly in some of the Greek city states in the last few centuries B.C.; and this is perhaps the reason why so many of us ardently love the Greeks of classical times. But in general the description is a fair one. It is certainly fair when applied to our own ancestors living in the centuries immediately before our modern days.

Their society was hierarchical; on the whole people accepted their "station" within it. When argument arose, it was not their habit to do as we would do—to appeal to reason, to examine the relevant facts in the outside world, to calculate future advantages one way or the other. They looked for precedents in the past and read ancient books to see what the authorities of olden times had to say about it. This (as I am told by those who have studied the matter closely) comes out very clearly, for example, in the arguments between our seventeenth-century parliamentarians and the early Stuart kings. Time and again the parliamentarians can be found hovering on the brink of arguments that would be the most natural thing in the world for any of us—arguments about the rights of the individual, about prosperity or expediency or social justice—and yet not quite able to utter them, and slipping back instead into a hopeless attempt to prove that they were only claiming what had been established by thirteenth- or fourteenth-century authority.

If this was the habit with political and social questions, how much more so with religious! In those days men's basic thought-patterns were such that they could accept an article of religious belief on the strength of someone else proclaiming it to them in an authoritative manner and with ample reference to the authoritative people who had believed it in time past. This does not mean that all men, all through that bygone age, would always accept anything that any missionary chose to say in a firm authoritative tone. There could be conflict of authority. Missionaries could be disbelieved; sometimes with unhappy consequences. The essential point is that in those days anyone could genuinely and sincerely accept something said with authority *without doing violence to the basic structure of his thinking*. He was not bound—was not conditioned by his deeply ingrained patterns of thought—to meet the authoritative proclamation with a challenge.

But we are. If someone tells us something remarkable, it is no use his ending with, "you can take it from me". Nor does it help him very much if he adds that enormous numbers of other people—or almost all people—have always believed something like it in the past. Our response, because of our basic thought-patterns, is bound to be: "It's no use your telling me what *you* believe, or what other people *have* believed; the question is whether *I* can be persuaded of it *now*?"

The adolescents who make this response in our Secondary Schools are not being perverse. They are obeying the whole spirit of the age in which we live; and, more significant, they are doing precisely what we are teaching them to do in our schools. In so far as we succeed in our deliberate efforts, the children are being taught not to accept anything merely because someone says so; but to examine the evidence, test the argument, and make up their own minds for themselves. This pragmatic attitude to life is immensely important; it is perhaps the greatest single thing we have in mind when we speak of our advancing into an egalitarian age. For this does not mean that all are equal in all respects; it need not even mean that all ought ideally to have the same pay; but it must mean that, so far as possible, each shall be free on fundamentals to make up his own mind. If this is not what we believe, we have no important common ground for our dislike of contemporary totalitarian practices.

All this is so inevitable for so many of us that we find it almost impossible to believe that there ever were men, women and adolescents for whom it was otherwise. But there were. Until quite recently there were very large numbers of people for whom someone else's proclamation was enough; it was enough that vast majorities had believed it for many centuries past. Their minds and hearts did not respond with an inevitable challenge.

We have said, too, that the age just ended was pre-scientific. This means far more than that the average citizen was then ignorant about the laws of science; after all, the majority of individual citizens are very nearly as ignorant even today. The point is that in those days men lived in a world in which nobody knew the laws of science. The world was not then known to be held together as a coherent and self-consistent entity by rules of cause-and-effect which operated in the same way every time they were put to practical test. Knowing, in our own days, that we have great numbers of scientists, and even of technologists, who know these rules, we have all given ourselves, as we have seen, a rough and ready test for separating the credible from the incredible. If it stems back to some machine, or to some mechanical process, which the technologists assure us conforms to the normal rules, then it is credible; if it doesn't, it isn't. The men of old times had no such test as this. In a very real sense anything could happen, with one thing being almost as likely as another.

It snowed. Why? No one really knew. So: "He sends the snow in winter." Water bubbled from a spring. Where from? No geologists drew them a sectional diagram showing the rock formations between the spring and the uplands where the water fell perhaps five or ten miles away. So a nymph was pushing it up. And when the supply failed, the nymph was angry and needed the right kind of propitiation. And if that failed, it showed there was something wrong with the ceremony. Why not?

It is not easy for us to believe that there was a day—in fact there was a long age—when adolescent boys and girls vividly believed in a world peopled with all kinds of queer beings—fairies, nymphs, angels, pixies, witches, devils, leprechauns and ghosts. No teacher was needed to give them these beliefs; the children sucked them up almost with their mothers' milk. When discussing the great effort that is needed in our day if we are to give any reality to the world invisible, P. W. Martin writes:

"In this effort of realisation, the present sophisticated age is at a considerable disadvantage compared with earlier times. Men of the classical times peopled the mountain tops with gods; while every meadow, fountain, grove and stream had its attendant nymphs and dryads, satyrs and fauns. During the Middle Ages, miracles were everywhere, angels and devils rubbed shoulders with men. As methods of realisation these were far from ideal. To our modern eyes they appear as so much childish superstition. But by concretising the world invisible they gave it a certain reality."[1]

How different in those days was the missionary's task from that which confronts the vicar on the twentieth-century housing estate. The missionary did not have to teach the people to believe. They believed already! His trouble was that they believed too much. He had to ask himself which of all their crazy notions he could allow them to go on believing and which of their queer practices he could sanctify with modest alterations. We know of a charming letter in which Gregory the Great instructs the Abbot Mellitus to convey a message on this subject to St. Augustine of Canterbury. He wrote:

> "The temples of the idols of that nation ought not to be destroyed; but let the idols that are in them be destroyed, let altars be erected and relics placed. . . . And because they have been used to slaughter many oxen in sacrifices to devils, some solemnity must be exchanged to them on this account as that, on the nativities of holy martyrs, they may build themselves huts of the boughs of trees, about those churches that have been turned to that use out of temples, and no more offer beasts to the Devil, but kill cattle to the praise of God . . . For there is no doubt that it is impossible to efface everything at once from their obdurate minds; because he who endeavours to ascend to the highest place, rises by degrees or steps, and not by leaps."[2]

The better known example, of course, is afforded by the missionaries who found German tribes worshipping their decorated oak trees. Instead of stopping them outright, they told their converts to change to fir trees and to do it only in mid-winter. The habit was introduced to Britain by Prince Albert just over a hundred and twenty years ago and is now indulged by almost all of us—the majority vaguely supposing that we are somehow doing something Christian.

But further consequences follow. From an early age our

[1] *Experiment in Depth*, (Routledge and Kegan Paul), p. 246. And see the reference to P. W. Martin in the Preface.

[2] *Bede's Ecclesiastical History* (Everyman Edition), pp. 52-3. In one or two places, as well as those indicated by dots, a few words have been omitted from the original.

fairly recent ancestors absorbed in their homes a firm belief in a world peopled with many queer beings who happened, almost by chance, to be invisible just now to the naked eye. When they learned to believe, as well, in One Supreme Being—in Jehovah of the Israelites or in the Christian God the Father—they had no difficulty whatever in visualising him with the inward eye as a very big man sitting up there amongst the clouds just beyond the sunset.

Once again, let us be clear that there was nothing in their pattern of thinking which positively obliged them to believe in any deity in any shape or form. In our age, which we often describe as atheist or agnostic, we probably underestimate the number of agnostics and atheists who lived at other times. And of course, then as now, there were the thousands who paid no more than lip service to their alleged religion. The important point is that if and in so far as men, women and children did believe in any Deity, their basic thought-patterns were not seriously upset, even in quite recent days, when they visualised God in their own minds as The Big Man.

There he was, in the stained glass window of the local church or more distant cathedral, glowing, glorious, mysterious, and sitting or standing or flying in gorgeous surroundings of some kind or other. The picture in the mind, the "image" of God (using the word in the modern technical sense), could be not very different—indeed not at all different—from the picture in the window.

A very large part of the language of the Church was fitted harmoniously—and to this very day it is still harmoniously fitted—to a God visualised in precisely this form.

> "By the overshadowing
> Of Thy gold and silver wing."

> "Casting down their golden crowns
> Around a glassy sea."

> "He sitteth at the right hand of God."

All the saints and mystics all the way down Christian history (or, as I should prefer to say, throughout the whole Childhood of the Christian Church) have always known perfectly well that

God does not have a wing; that immortal spirits do not wear crowns; and even that God has no right hand at which anyone may sit. Saints and mystics have interpreted these, and a thousand comparable phrases, as poetic allegory, or glorious symbolic picture language to be said or sung or prayed so as to convey to human heart a feeling, an idea, an aspiration dimly corresponding to a reality utterly different from anything that could be understood by any pedestrian and literalistic interpretation of each word in its normal mundane meaning.

All perfectly true; but suppose that some devil's advocate had one day tackled the saint or mystic on the propriety of offering this kind of language to the masses. "All very well," the advocate might have said, "for you and the rest of a tiny minority to revel in your allegorical interpretations. What about the majority? You are offering this very same language to them; and as you know perfectly well, they are not interpreting it at all, let alone allegorically. They take it straight. You are telling them that God has wings, that God sits down with someone on his right, that around some kind of lake the departed dead doff crowns of gold. What sort of saint are you to delude these simple souls with known untruth?"

And how might the saint have replied?

"You have said that these are simple people and so they are. They are not lifted very far above the ignorance, the naked barbarism, from which their forefathers emerged not many generations ago. They are as yet incapable of allegorical interpretation. But remember: No words, no phrases, no interpretations can express the inexpressible truth of God. These words, these phrases, taken straight, are all that these people can now receive. So taken, so received, these phrases lift these people, by a little, nearer to the Truth."

Or, shortening it: "These phrases, taken straight, are the best we can do just now."

It would have been a fair answer. And with modest obvious alterations it would be fair justification for the way we offer the truth today in Primary Schools and Sunday Schools to children who are recapitulating the pre-scientific stage of human evolution.

But our whole community is now moving into a new stage; and by the time each child reaches his own personal adolescence, he begins to be aware of it, even if only at an almost subconscious level. God, as is His custom, has not done our work for us; nor has He spared us the pain and frustration and the whole process of agonising endeavour which constitute the very anvil on which our souls are hammered into shape. He has not handed us a new generation of adolescents with the interpretative faculties that marked the saints and mystics of Church history. But the Holy Spirit has lead into our Secondary Schools, perhaps only in the last couple of generations, a company of teenagers who cannot any longer take these old words and phrases straight.

There are other aspects of the great change in basic thought-patterns that have to be considered—some of them perhaps rather harder to elucidate and grasp. For example, our ancestors in a bygone age had not yet isolated Reason from the other faculties as we have today. In one sense—and in a perfectly proper sense too—they were nothing like so reasonable as we are. In any number of books on the Middle Ages, the authors ask us to think of the men and women of those times as children—good children and bad, hardworking and lazy, prudent and foolish—but always as children. And pre-adolescent children at that!

Now this is most important. Anyone who has watched primary school children at their work and play knows perfectly well that reason is not absent from their being. On the contrary, to problems at a suitable level of difficulty, reason is quite vigorously applied. Yet, at that age, for all the important new items of knowledge-experience that any child is grasping month after month and day after day, the child himself does not consciously distinguish between that which is grasped through reason alone, through intuition alone, through experience alone, through imagination alone. Each new piece of life and truth is grasped, as far as the child is concerned, with his Whole Being.

In this sense, irrespective of what we choose to put before them by way of religious instruction, the children in the Primary Schools are inescapably recapitulating the living experience of the authoritarian, pre-scientific muscle-driven stage of evolution.

But our adolescents are not like that. Already, by the age of twelve or thirteen, they begin to be affected by the spirit of our age—and the greater their intelligence and vitality and integrity, the more surely they are affected by it. Several centuries of triumphant rationalism—using that word in all its noblest and most glorious meanings—have led us to isolate Reason from the other faculties of perception, and to give it such a place that nothing seems acceptable unless it commends itself and establishes itself, beyond possibility of rational disputation, to Reason alone.

This, then, is perhaps the deeper meaning of that saying of Jesus that no one can enter the Kingdom of Heaven unless he will receive it "as a little child". This does not mean that we have to go back and accept again a pre-rational state of authoritarian superstition. It means that we have to go on, with Reason unimpaired, past the isolation of Reason, so as to discover our Whole Being. This is a point to which we shall have to return.

Related to the isolation of Reason has been the virtual disappearance from amongst us of any sense of Sin. It may very well be argued that our ancestors were held too fiercely in its grip; that they were self-damagingly grim and morbid about it. Be that as it may, and be the causes of it whatever they may have been, the fact remains that each one of them who started thinking seriously about himself at all, knew—in a phrase from William James's classic summary—that there was "something wrong with him as he naturally stood".[1] And he knew it in his bones; he did not need to be specially instructed.

Now we have "escaped" from all this. We think of ourselves as reasonable, not always bothering to realise that this may only mean that we cannot help giving ourselves respectable-sounding

[1] From *Varieties of Religious Experience*. The whole of this summary will become important for our argument on page 163 below.

"reasons" for whatever our self-centred emotions have decided to do or leave undone. If we are ever conscious of serious wrong, we regard it as exceptional; or find ways of deciding that it was not really our fault. It was environment, or the ill-consequence of unfortunate childhood, or heredity. In short, in half-baked form, we have gobbled up from the psychologists the things that help us to treat life flippantly, without as yet having begun to learn from them the things that might show us how to take it seriously.

Our ancestors were different. However crude their ideas about Sin, they learned from them that it was advisable to take quite a serious view of Life. They had, by nature, a strongly felt need, at any rate, for "Something".

But there is a still further point, perhaps more important and at the same time more difficult than any that have gone before. It is a question of subtracting from our consciousness something so utterly integral to the whole, something permeating and colouring it all so intimately, that we are virtually unaware of its separate existence and can hardly conceive what it would be like to be without it. By contrast, it is comparatively easy to form some idea of what it must be like to be blind; one only needs to try to dress and shave with one's eyes shut; and even at that, a blind man would surprise one in a score of ways by mentioning aspects of blindness that had not revealed themselves in the simple experiment. Now try the experiment of imagining what it would be like to be deprived of Individualism!

At first the suggestion sounds meaningless.

But we know, as a matter of fact, that all the interrelated ideas and feelings about ourselves and about each other, which we now subsume under the title "Individualism", have all emerged into active human consciousness slowly and relentlessly in the course of the last few hundred years. The complicated and many-sided process is traced in such classics as R. H. Tawney's *Religion and the Rise of Capitalism* and Professor Macmurray's *Clue to History*, and in scores of other works. But if something has emerged through a complicated process, then clearly, before the process started, there must have beeen a time when it was not there. At least, it was not there at anything like its present sharp level of realisation.

So what is this Individualism? As I am a socialist in contemporary British politics, it naturally follows that in my judgment this Individualism has now led us into one or two regretable mental habits and value judgments. But this is trivial. A twentieth-century democratic socialist is perfectly capable of appreciating the wonderful flowering of the human spirit that this dynamic word describes. Indeed, in one sense, one could take Columbus, Copernicus and Luther and the vast process that they symbolise, and describe the whole thing as man's discovery of Individualism. It is the individual becoming acutely aware of his own separate reality *vis-à-vis* the community; his claim to express his personality by thinking and doing for himself—exploring alike new lands, new realms of thought, new ways of looking for truth, new means of expressing it; it is the individual's firm claim to live his own life. And in the egalitarian community, it is our common acceptance of the fact that we have no right simply to disregard, still less to liquidate, any minority however small. The whole process is essentially glorious; and there can never be any question of our willingly going back on it.

But there was a day when it had not yet happened. There was a day when ordinary men, women and children did not know and feel all that we know and feel so intimately that we can hardly imagine what life was like without it.

What does all this mean for religion?

Religion—whether the crude religion of the barbarian or the exalted religion of the saint—ultimately "lives" at the level of a man's deep ideas and feelings about himself, and about his relatedness to all the other people, to Life as a whole, and to whatever Being or beings exist behind Life's outward show. In the heyday of the age that has now ended, men, women and children were religious in a way that we are not—and this not because we have sunk below their social level, but because, as we have just seen, we have spent the last few centuries struggling forward beyond it. Without the need for any kind of instruction, without having to think conscious thoughts, "without questions asked", they felt themselves to be integrally linked and related to each other in all kinds of tribal and feudal ways. Their social solidarity, compared by St. Paul and by medieval churchmen to the solidarity of the eye and the toe with each other and with the rest of the body, still had an appreciable kinship with sheer animal gregariousness which we have been progressively transcending in our sharp realisation of our individual personalities.

Now the men, women and children who had so little difficulty in feeling—indeed, simply could not help themselves from feeling—so closely integrated with each other and with the whole community, had equally little difficulty in feeling themselves livingly related to the whole of Life and to the Being or beings that might stand behind it thinly veiled from naked eye-sight. They may have felt and expressed this relationship in childish, superstitious or sometimes in loathsome ways; but they felt it as something unchallengeably real. And all this by nature, and without specific instruction of any kind.

Christian teachers in those days did not have to start out by helping the people to know what it meant to have a religious outlook. They knew it already. Or rather—and much more important and far harder for us to grasp—they did not *know* that they had it; they just simply *had* it so fundamentally that they did not consciously know that they had it, since the state of being in which one might not have it was simply inconceivable to them. In such a situation, the Christian missionary could properly start with:

> "These people are already essentially religious. Their present religion is false. I shall go straight ahead and tell them the religion that is true."

In any particular case the missionary might be believed and reverenced, or disbelieved and eaten; but either way his starting-point was correct.

Let it be clear, once again, that there is no question of going back. We cannot retrace our steps into the almost herd-like relatedness of human community as it was in olden days. Individualism has given each the chance and the right and the burdensome duty of standing on his own feet and making up his own mind for himself. But "the other side of the penny" is that Individualism has also lead each of us to think of himself, and to "feel" himself, standing out over against the community, against the others, isolated from them, in no sense integrated with them or with the totality of Life.

Now the almost instinctive relatedness of members of earlier communities did not necessarily constitute a truly religious outlook on life; still less was it equivalent to the whole Christian faith. But it was an important part of both; and in a bygone age men, women and adolescents had this important part "by nature". Similarly, our feeling of separatedness from the others, from the herd, from Life in general, does not necessarily involve any one of us in bloody-mindedness. But, *in default of rather careful and deliberate instruction*, it can easily be a long step towards it.

Then let us summarise: They were authoritarian by nature; they lived in a community where no one knew that there were Laws of Nature; one thing was as likely as another; they had no difficulty in believing in all kinds of gods and godlings, nor in visualising the Supreme God as a Big Man in the Sky.

They made their childish decisions with the Whole Being, whereas we tend to make our more sophisticated judgments by and through Reason alone.

They had a built-in sense of Sin; we insist that we are reasonable, so that if anything goes wrong we think of ourselves as victims rather than cause of what happens.

They had a natural and almost instinctive relatedness to Life as a whole; we have a natural and almost instinctive sense of isolation from it.

Taking all the points together, they constitute quite a formidable change of outlook. In one sense the change has not come quickly. If we could go back three or four centuries and apply the necessary sociological tests, we should surely find minorities breaking away from the old outlook and beginning to adopt the new; and these minorities would include many of the most intelligent, the most dynamic, or, in a word, many of the leading members of their several generations. But if we are thinking, not of leading minorities, but of the great mass of the homes from which our secondary school children are now drawn, then it may very well be that it is only within the last couple of generations that the old outlook has been thoroughly thrown off and the new outlook thoroughly put on.

Taking the situation as a whole, it would seem to go a long way to explain a sentence that is printed in bold on the back outside cover of Harold Loukes's *Teenage Religion*:

> "Three-quarters of Britain's children are educated in the nation's secondary modern schools. There they receive religious instruction, and take part in acts of worship. **Then they enter a society which has virtually cut itself off from religion."**

There seems to be but one possible criticism of this judgment. "Then" implies that the children enter the God-forsaken Society only when they leave school. This is not so. They have been living in it, absorbing all its semiconscious assumptions, thinking their thoughts in accordance with its basic thought-patterns, ever since they came into the Secondary School.

In the light of all this it would seem rather a moderate conclusion that revolutionary change in religious teaching methods may now be required.

CHAPTER SIX

THE APPROACH TO THE NEW SITUATION

THE TEACHER WILL have to come into the open and explain to the class that he intends a radical change in religious teaching.

After all, the classroom situation, as we have seen, is telling the children: "Sit up and listen, and you will get your Christianity from teacher's penny packets." Either the children will notice a definite change, or they will not. If they do not, the situation will continue to stamp the theological untruth into their hearts.[1] If they do notice it, they are entitled to some explanation.

On top of this, no teacher will go very far along the lines suggested in the next few chapters without being challenged by the children with: "Look here, Sir, this isn't what the Church tells us." The challenge may not be backed by any direct quotation of anything that may have been said or written by any particular priest or minister. And the teenagers may be wrong in the sense that many of the following pages will be filled with the simple suggestion that we should actually start teaching children some of the things that have been perfectly well known to the best minds in the Church for perhaps the last couple of generations. But the children will be right in so far as they will be speaking of the "image" of the Church and of the Church's teaching which will have been built up in their minds from goodness knows where—very often from the whole background atmosphere that they breathe in their homes. In this sense what the teacher has to say to them is bound to seem different, and sometimes opposite, from that which they believe has been said to them by the Church as a whole.

Nor have we quite finished. There is something else that has to be explained to the adolescents by anyone who asks them

[1] See pages 50-52 above.

seriously to confront religion in general and Christianity in particular in this second half of the twentieth century; something obvious and important which can, none-the-less, be quietly "forgotten" at primary stage because either the children do not then notice it, or for some queer reason at that stage it does not seem to worry them. But at secondary stage it cannot be ignored, because the children have noticed it, and it does worry them either at the conscious or (more damaging) at the semiconscious level of thought and feeling. And yet, unless I am badly mistaken, the "average" R.E. teacher blandly soldiers on with his secondary teaching without one single reference to this staggering fact ever crossing his lips. He never refers to the fact that a good majority of the adolescents' mothers, aunts and older sisters and an absolutely overwhelming majority of their fathers, uncles and older brothers, do not display the smallest concern for religion from end to end of the normal week.

Surely this majestic fact cannot be simply ignored by anyone who talks to adolescents about religion? Does it not need to be explained? And do we not find, in the fact that it is not explained, a basic cause of the teacher's complaint that the children are not interested. "It might be all right," says the well-intentioned but exasperated teacher, "if only they'd get up and argue back; but they just sit like puddings, not interested one way or the other!"

Why should they be? Teacher stands there saying it matters; the whole outside world says it does not. And teacher does not seem to know. Teacher prattles on as if the outside world did not exist. Teacher does not even seem to be living in the real world where we have to get out and work in about eighteen months' time. Why *should* we be interested in teacher's sham world?

And which of two alternative impressions to we want to establish in the adolescents' minds. Do we want them to have the impression that we are saying: "Your fathers and uncles are dead wrong. The Church is and always has been right. It is time you woke up and acknowledged this fact by coming back to the Church." Or would it be better if they understood us to say: "Had your fathers and uncles been slightly more perceptive, they might have found religious truth despite the Church. Nevertheless it is partly the fault of out-of-date teaching that they did not do so. And as you look at them, do they seem to have found either peace or purpose in their lives without religion? And as we are going to try to learn about it differently, is it not perhaps worth paying attention?"

If we are concerned for the dignity of the Church we shall doubtless hope to sustain the first of these alternatives; but if we are concerned for Christ, who can doubt that we should aim to establish the second.

Very well, then; if I may dare say so without too much immodesty, it is all in Chapter Two. The facts leading to the need for a revolution were not offered only to the teacher as a preliminary justification for proposed teaching changes to be suggested later on. These are basic facts which must be taught to the class as the foundation without which all that follows will be built on sand.

Nor is there likely to be any serious difficulty.

Interest will be aroused because the class will have been told, by the R.E. teacher, that they are going to spend three or four weeks (or perhaps rather less if the class agrees to throw in "their" discussion period each week as well) so as to learn why the Church has gone wrong. The whole thing can be worked out as a time chart. Each child can make his own on a strip of paper tape to some such scale as five centimetres per thousand years. But a communal effort on a larger scale would be much better.[1] When finished the whole time chart can be strung out around the room as a frieze; or "snaked" back and forth over a more compact pin-up space. Either way, names of outstanding events and pioneers may be added in appropriate places; and the children should be asked to collect pictures of olden times and of modern technology to illustrate the different periods. These, of course, will be spread rather sparsely along the first few yards, and crammed together, one overlapping another, around the last few inches.

[1] Actually it is best to "cheat" with the scale quite openly. For example, 5″ per millennium to about 5000 B.C.; 10″ per millennium from then to the birth of Christ; 2″ per century up to A.D. 1700; then 1″ per decade until A.D. 2000. This gives about twenty feet in all.

But at the end of the process, the teacher can stand at the chart and open up the dear old blackboard compass to point to the period before 1750 with: "Don't you see! The whole human race is still in process of coming out of *that* age and is only just beginning to look around and find its feet in *this* age. What the Church says to you—or, to be a little more accurate, what you think you hear the Church saying to you—is largely old echoes of what the Church used to be saying to the people of that age. What the Church then said to those people wasn't wrong. It was right, for those people. But the world has changed—not slowly in the kind of way in which it was always slowly changing even back in those centuries over there—but here, in these last inches, it has changed suddenly and out of all recognition. And people's minds have suddenly changed with it. Your minds, the minds of your mothers and fathers, are clean different from men's minds even a hundred years ago. And with the new state of mind, the old words and the old pictures that the Church used in those old days, won't do any more."

With any normal luck the teacher will be in a room giving a view (or at least a glimpse) of some part of a town or suburb, so that at the window he can say: "And so, in those houses over there, and in thousands of others like them all the way from Land's End to John o' Groats, you've got people who throw away the old words and the old pictures. Quite right. But the tragedy is that they turn their backs on the unchanging Truth as well—Truth which the old words and old pictures showed well enough to the people of *that* age—Truth that still needs to be known by the children, and by the grown-ups, in *this* age. But it isn't known. And that's why the world of those houses over there is such a God-forsaken place for you children to be growing up into.

"Now you've got another two and a half terms with me twice a week; and in that time you're going to hear a good deal which will seem to be different from what you think you have heard from the Church as a whole. And we have made this chart, and you have brought those pictures, so that we can see why."

The teacher may be further challenged with the question

whether Christians have any right to change their language, to broaden their ideas and bring their message up to date. We met this challenge before; and we saw what Professor Whitehead had to say about it.[1] But how can we convey such lofty sentiments as his to twelve or thirteen-year-old children? Difficult, or course, but not impossible. It could be done, for example, by a fairly simple adaptation of a blackboard diagram that must be well known to many teachers. Basically one makes a drawing of a sectional view through a stairway beginning bottom left and leading to a broad level landing which runs out about three-quarters of the way up the right-hand edge of the board. The steps are dated, and each is given the name of an Old Testament patriarch or prophet together with the shortest possible statement of his conception of God; thus "2000 B.C., Abraham, Tribal God; 1250, Moses, Covenant God; 860, Elijah, Israel's God; 760, Amos, Righteous God; 740, Hosea, Loving God; 720, Isaiah, Holy God; 620, Jeremiah, Personal God; 550, 2nd Isaiah, Universal God." On the top step, which forms the beginning of the level landing, stands the Cross.[2] As a first introduction to the sequence of the prophets, as a scaffolding on which to hang deepening knowledge, as a visual representation of the way in which the whole prophetic message leads up to Christ, I think most teachers will agree that it cannot be bettered. As it stands, however, with nothing beyond the Cross except the rest of that broad level landing, it runs the risk of reinforcing, does it not, our "finished-and-done-with-and-mustn't-be-altered-any-more" attitude to religious Truth. By all means let the Cross stand on a broader step than any of the others; let the whole outline of the stairway change colour as we pass from B.C. to A.D. But let us have another step dated A.D. 1300-1600. For a name, "Wycliffe"; and for our summary phrase, "Bible for all".

And so to the last step—at any rate the last that we know

[1] See page 30 above.

[2] See *A Book of Bible Activities*, Norman J. Bull (Hulton), p. 16. The author is a colleague of mine to whom I am indebted for much friendship and generous advice. He points out that the diagram is necessarily a simplification; and that it would better represent the truth if the process were shown as a section, not through a rigid stairway, but through an ascending range of mountain peaks, each prophet-peak higher than the last. I persist in regarding the more simplified version as an excellent way of linking the prophets.

anything about. We may date it A.D. 1860-2160; and because we are only part way up it, we must begin the riser with a solid line which must soon break into a series of dashes of diminishing length until the tread, on which it will not be given to us to stand in this mortal life, is represented by a line of dots. If we must have a name, let us write "Darwin"! And for a summary: "Baptism of Science".

This phrase must be explained to the class in its double meaning. It means, on the one hand, that all our religious knowledge is to be deepened and expanded, and all our old religious language is to be reinterpreted and changed by all the new truth made known to men by the Holy Spirit through the work of all the scientists, past present and future. It also means that all the staggering new knowledge brought to light by the scientists is to be baptised in the Truth of God that does not change at all, even in times when men suddenly see more of it and need to express it in new words and phrases. Through the operation of this process of mutual baptism we may hope to see the way out of the dilemma stated by Samuel Butler more than a hundred years ago when he said:

> "The men of religion tell a lot of little lies for the sake of one big truth and the men of science tell a lot of little truths for the sake of one big lie."[1]

If the suggested diagram were first done on the board in coloured chalk, a group of children might do it out large and neat on a big sheet of cartridge paper to be pinned on the wall either permanently, or during Religion and Life Discussion Periods. And (particularly if some of the children could be introduced to a typewriter) the steps might be gradually decorated with "balloons" giving some of the startling words from the prophets involved in the earlier steps, and from some of the men and women who are helping us up the step that is still uncompleted.

If the teacher is challenged by one of the adolescents who wants to know why, in all these circumstances, they were taught "baby stuff" in Primary School, then he must take

[1] Quoted from D. C. Somervell's *Disraeli and Gladstone* (Jarrolds), p. 129.

three or four weeks to teach them (or to remind them) about the basic facts of evolution; and about the need for each human being to recapitulate all the stages. It will be a good thing, in any case, to teach evolution during the Religion and Life Discussion Periods.

Assuming, then, that we agree to explain to the children that a change in teaching is being made, and why we are making it, let us examine, as methodically as possible, the differences between the basic thought-patterns that were prevalent in olden days and those that have become general during the last very few generations; and let us see what alterations in teaching methods are called for by each.

We might begin from the fact that we meet, for the first time, great masses of adolescents who come from homes where it is no longer possible to visualise God anthropomorphically—to see him, that is to say, as the Big Man in the Sky. There is really very little to be said about it except, perhaps, to defend this part of the whole theme against any critic who might say that it is all out of date because the Church as a whole understands the situation perfectly and is dealing with it satisfactorily. Anyone inclined to agree with such criticism might perhaps read *Return to Belief* by Yvonne Lubbock—a remarkable book containing, as its title implies, the story of how one woman found her way back to Christian faith.

The important points for our present purpose are that Yvonne Lubbock seems to have found her way without any help from anyone in the Church; and that she had been driven from Christian belief *by the Church*! Speaking of the time when she was beginning to read Hegel, she writes:

> "In spite of my will I began to see a meaning behind the metaphors; to realise that it was against the literalisation that I had rebelled and not against the philosophical ideas themselves since the Church did not bother to give us the living ideas behind the bare dogmas. It was not surprising that

dogma slept or was as dead as a skeleton. Why did the Church allow men to remain tied to their picture-thinking, which was tantamount to dragging a corpse around? It was small wonder that any self-reflecting mind cut itself loose from such a burden. But need there have been a corpse? If the Church had given men the inner meaning behind the mere outer expression of dogma, that might have been no dead burden but a living truth that could have born fruit in the human spirit. Not once during my co-called Christian days had I heard the Church warn against the abuse of metaphors; and such was my malevolence towards it in my agnostic period that I assumed that it had introduced doctrine in order to be esoteric and give itself importance as the sole interpreter of such cryptograms."[1]

It may be said that the period referred to as "my so-called Christian days" may well have been several decades ago. But intellectual phenomena work slowly down the ladder of intellectual perception; and if someone as mentally alert as Mrs. Lubbock was being driven from Christ in this way in her early days, it is virtually certain that teenagers in our Secondary Schools are being driven from Him today by the same Christian teachers' failure. At bottom it is a failure to see that we are falling between two stools. No longer do we have the masses who could take the old language straight; not yet do we have the generations who learn the art of allegorical interpretation at their mothers' knees.

Any teacher who recognises the situation and has the serious will to tackle it, should find no difficulty in principle. He will take pains to put as little as possible of the old anthropomorphic language under the adolescents' noses. In so far as he cannot hope to conceal all of it from all of them, he will take the initiative in categorically ordering them not to take it straight. If at any moment with any group he cannot go further, at least let him say:

"This old stuff suited men of old time; it is venerable in its way; there are some worthy people who rather like the

[1] *Op. cit.* (Collins), p. 139.

flavour of it even now. But for the time being, it is not for you; nor will it be until we have found time to put in some special instruction about how to translate it into modern language."

And this, of course, points obviously to the third and last stage. With advanced groups, the teacher may begin to give training and practice in allegorical interpretation. For example:

Write out in modern English the truth that may be allegorically understood from:

"*The Father on his sapphire throne*
Awaits his own anointed Son."

But the present mischief is not confined to anthropomorphic words and phrases that can no longer be taken straight and are not yet allegorically interpreted. Thousands are today allowed to stumble over the beliefs which they suppose the Church to be requiring them to believe—and this irrespective of the quality of the language in which the beliefs are expressed.

We saw that in an earlier day great masses of people, without the need for special instruction, believed too much. Their minds were stuffed with odd notions about queer beings who had to be propitiated through a whole tangle of strange practices. By contrast, without special instruction and because of the whole tone and quality of contemporary society, the children of our day start by believing nothing.

We saw, too that in olden days, when men believed too much, one of the missionary's first jobs was to decide how many of their existing beliefs and practices might reasonably be retained; for it was important, in the first instance, to raise the minimum obstruction against the inflow of essential Truth. Writing of the struggles of the early Church in our own country, Arthur Bryant says:

"Its philosophy of love and forgiveness was not easily grasped by men whose forebears had offered sacrifices to demons. In converting successive waves of heathen, the Church had allowed them to cling to many foolish fancies so long as they accepted the truth that Christ, the Son of God, loved mankind and had died for the remission of its sins."[1]

The same basic problem remains. We must raise the minimum obstruction against the inflow of essential Truth. Let it not be too great a shock. When children started by believing too much, one of the first jobs was to tell them how much they might go on believing. Now that they start by believing nothing, the corresponding task is to *make sure that they know how much they do not have to start believing*!

Nor can we accept any teacher's complaint that "*I* never told them they had to believe So-and-So." Perhaps he didn't; but the whole situation, assisted, as we shall see in a moment, by the "Devil" as well, is shouting that the Church does indeed require them to believe all kinds of things; and they will usually go on accepting what they have absorbed from the situation unless the teacher can positively and very clearly instruct them in something different.

First, then, let us consider all that is involved in the old battle between Church and Science. Do people still believe that a Christian—the sort of man or woman who goes to Church—is also the sort who thinks that everything in the Old Testament is true in the ordinary and everyday meaning of that word?

At the level of the university senior common room the battle is over, and has been for years. And doubtless there are amongst us a good many twelve-year-olds for whom it now presents no difficulties. The four boys referred to above on page 42 are examples.

But are such boys typical of their whole generation? Is the whole *Church versus Science* battle all finished and done with? I have often been told that it is—and not only by men and women who have no experience at secondary school level.

[1] *Makers of the Realm* (Collins), p. 209.

I am bound, therefore, to deploy such evidence as has come to me.

In my last year at Wandsworth, my senior set prefect was one of the most dedicated young men I have ever met. One day, as if it were the most natural thing in the world, he came out with: "Of course, Sir, I can't be a Christian because the Church is against Science." Nor is it enough to shrug this off with: "Well, that's just one boy." This boy, so alert and intelligent, could not have said this thing unless the whole social atmosphere in which he lives had given it to him to say.

From one of our minor public schools a science master who is also a Christian told me: "The boys are astonished to find a Christian teaching science; they think it's against nature."

Since starting to write this book, I had a chance of talking to the top form of a Plymouth Secondary School on "What sort of world is this, anyway?" When most left, five boys and four girls remained to ask more questions and, amongst others, the following interchange took place:

> "Excuse me, Sir, you was talking about religion at the end of what you said?"
>
> "Well, yes; I think you might fairly say that I did work round to that subject."
>
> "Ah. Well, I've just about decided to give it up."
>
> "That's not necessarily fatal; I did much the same thing at about your age. But can you say what's the trouble?"
>
> "Well, Sir, it's this Adam and Eve. I mean to say, Sir, in biology we learn . . ."

On the very weekend after which my typescript must leave me to be set up in print, I am sent a remarkable piece of research carried out by Ronald Goldman of Reading University and published in September 1962. I only wish I had known of it sooner so as to digest it all while my own argument was still fluid. But amongst Goldman's conclusions I find:

> "It is evident from the Biblical concepts reviewed that no real awareness of the nature of the Bible is grasped until well into the secondary school course, and even here the Bible is regarded as authoritative in a strongly literal sense. It appears

that pupils are not aware of the possibility of a critical but reverent approach to Scripture."[1]

Naturally I tried to discover the attitude of the seventeen fifth formers who have been mentioned on page 17 above. Colleagues to whom I have described my effort have dismissed it as valueless on the ground that it created the answers it wanted. I shall therefore describe it, so that it may be judged.

The boys already had bits of paper on which they had been invited not to write their names. I said:

> "There is a dispute. It is not about God, or whether He exists, or what He's like; nor about morals or anything about how men ought to behave. It's just about what you might call a plain matter of fact—the age of rocks, whether the sun or the world came into existence first, whether some king lived here or there, at this date or that. And on this plain factual dispute, the Bible says one thing and Science says something different. Which is right?"

The papers, when collected, rather surprised me by showing that only fourteen out of seventeen unreservedly backed Science; two gave qualified, and one gave absolute support to the Bible. But in the meanwhile, we had gone on:

> "The second question is harder. I want you to imagine a Brains Trust up here. Freddie Grisewood is in the chair; and on the panel a bishop, a Roman Catholic father, a Free Church minister and a churchwarden. And, by chance, the first one invited to ask a question is me; and up I get and ask that Brains Trust the very same question that I have just asked you."

The question was repeated verbatim, and play-acted as if to a Brains Trust in a public hall.

> "All right; the members of the panel give their answers; and last of all the question master sums up."

In case of doubt, I enlarged on the functions of the question master at this final stage, and continued:

[1] *Some Aspects of the Development of Religious Thinking in Childhood and Adolescence* (Department of Education, Reading University), p. 44.

"Now, will you think about it; try to imagine that you are in that audience listening; imagine what the members of the panel will say to this question of ours. And now will you write what you think Freddie Grisewood would have to say in his summing-up?"

Here are most of the answers: "Without doubt they would say the Bible is correct and the scientists are in the wrong." "If this question were asked, we should get something like two-thirds for the Bible and one-third for the scientists because they would say that they were both related in some way." "I think three of the brains trust would say the Bible and the last would say the scientist. Those who said the Bible I feel would believe in something of what the scientist says but mostly what the Bible says." "They would probably say the Bible is right because they were all members of the Church. If they were more broad minded it would be difficult to draw a conclusion." "They would be in agreement that the Bible is right." "Being members of the Church, they say the Bible." "I would expect them to say that the Brains Trust was unanimous on the point and the Lord Above created it. This decision is more definite with the Bishop and the Roman Catholic than with the church-warden and the free minister." "In our opinion the Bible would be right, but then again the scientist would be right, so in other words we don't quite know." "They would say that the Bible is right due to the fact that clergymen, the majority of the panel, tend to disregard anything said against church teaching." "These people would all be sure that the Bible is right, as it is their belief, making the scientist completely wrong." I omit a small number who said quite briefly, in effect: "They say the Bible's right." About three gave no answer.

I stand subject to correction; but I cannot see that these answers can be dismissed as valueless. Several members of the class were at that time in a mood to sauce me if they had found ways of doing it. And what, in my procedure, biased them against giving some such answer as:

"What century do you think you're living in? Anyone of any intelligence knows perfectly well that on questions of this kind the Church has long since accepted what the scientists say."

This, or something like it, would have been the correct answer if teachers in class and pulpit were effectively presenting the twentieth-century Christian truth.

And yet, when all this has been said, there remains the feeling that something queer is working against us. I recall, for example, that the head of the R.E. department at Wandsworth was a passionate anti-fundamentalist; and yet his sound Christian faith somehow did not get through to that senior set prefect. Whole libraries of books have set out the contemporary Truth. Fifteen years ago, to my certain knowledge, the Exeter Diocesan Sunday School Association, in printed teachers notes, was recommending George Barclay's *Making and Meaning of the Bible*, in which he wrote as long ago as 1923:

> "It is necessary to be quite frank about the conclusion to which we are driven. Adam and Eve and Cain and Abel are not historical persons who lived the kind of life described in the Bible. There was no actual man called Noah from whom the whole human race took its rise a second time. The Garden of Eden is not to be located in any actual part of the world, Mesopotamia or elsewhere, and there never was, sitting at its gate, an angel with a flaming sword. Cain was not an actual man who married a wife at a time when there were no other women on earth except his mother, nor was he an actual man who was afraid of being murdered at a time when the only other man on earth was his father. There never was a serpent who spoke to a woman in words of human speech."[1]

And, as we saw, George Adam Smith was treating the Book of Jonah as inspired parable in 1896. Yet it does not seem to get through. Why not?

Of course there is the fear of trouble. This means that many clergymen and R.E. teachers who think themselves quite up-to-date, would find, if their words were tape-recorded and carefully analysed, that on this subject they are doing no more

[1] *Op. cit.* (S.C.M.), p. 49.

than admitting that the Church no longer quarrels with the conclusions of scientists in their proper field. This will never cut any ice. If something contrary to the presuppositions of our whole social atmosphere has to be learned, it is no use to *admit* it; it has to be *proclaimed*! And the difficulty is that educated Christians are unlikely to take any action if the teacher does not proclaim the sharp contemporary truth; whereas members of a dozen queer sects are all too likely to protest if he does. This, at any rate, seemed to be the headmaster's explanation for the sad ignorance of the boy I met in Plymouth.

But there is something more. The fact is that the Devil is working overtime against us on this part of the front.

To avoid misunderstanding, may I say that whenever the Devil is mentioned in this book he is to be interpreted allegorically; because when interpreted in this sense, I believe in him passionately, though seldom, I fear, as vigilantly as I ought. Allegorically, then, the Devil knows perfectly well that his whole cause is safe as long as he can shield from all challenge the slovenly unexamined state of mind that made that set prefect say that the Church is against Science. Coming out of the language of religious allegory and into the jargon of modern psychology, we are meeting here a first-class example of the psychological phenomenon known as rationalisation. The fact is that in the first instance and with the conscious parts of their minds, most adolescents do not want to be Christians. They may be vaguely aware of something down in their own depths trying to tell them that in the end Christ could put purpose and peace into their lives. But in the beginning, becoming a Christian would mean, amongst other things, quarter of an hour earlier out of bed in the morning so as to make time to pray. No one wants to say to himself: "The reason I am not a Christian is that I'm a physical sluggard and have so little present concern, even for my own long-term deepest harmony, let alone for anyone else in the whole wide world, that I'm just not prepared to make the smallest effort in moral self-discipline." In fact, almost everyone is almost compelled to find some way of never seriously saying to himself anything of the kind. The way of escape is through rationalisation—the process by which we find something (indeed anything) that we can pass off on ourselves as an intellectually respectable reason for not doing the things that we just don't want to do anyway. And of all the contemporary rationalisations for closing one's heart and mind against the possibility of Christian Truth, there has never been a handier or more obvious one than: "Christian? Not me! Why; the Church is against Science!" That hard worn analogy about pouring water on a duck's back is a pretty apt description of what happens when anyone tries to teach anything which, if accepted, would smash up one of these cosy rationalisations.

Teachers in pulpit or classroom should therefore know that an occasional politely correct admission will get us nowhere. We must go into battle joyfully—"all flags flying and all guns firing", so to speak—against the appalling state of contemporary error.

And if any teacher ends up in some kind of public row, then bully for him! It is an astonishing fact that a large proportion of the avowed servants of Christ have somehow persuaded themselves that a first requirement for modern discipleship is to keep out of public controversy! A rip-roaring public row on this issue, with press headlines and deputations of protest, and the bishop obliged to take sides openly either for the Inter-Varsity Fellowship or for the Truth—all this would do the cause of Christ more good in a week than all the sermons preached in the average diocese in a twelvemonth. And if any teacher finds himself on the brink of trouble, let him take courage. Rationalisation, the Devil and the Plymouth Brethren may be against him; but thank God, Dr. William Temple, lately Archbishop of Canterbury, is on his side.

And this brings us to *Doctrine in the Church of England* published by S.P.C.K. for ten and six.

For nearly a quarter of a century I have been periodically expressing my amazement that this report is so little known. If the Nottingham Institute of Education invites me to a conference specially to consider Christian education, and if there be some sixty-five teachers and eight clergymen present, then even in this very specialised audience, I find that about three of the clergy and four of the teachers have heard of the book. I really cannot understand how it has been possible, for so many years, to inhibit the explosion of this spiritual warhead.

I well remember lending the report, in 1944, to one of my colleagues on the executive committee of the war-time movement called Common Wealth. He was, and is, one of the most dedicated servants of humanity that I know; but he has left the Christian Church into which he was baptised and confirmed. The exact words that passed when I got the book back have long slipped from memory; but their purport remains as clear as day.

"I never knew, Richard, that any Church Commission could write so much good sense."

"Wonderful; and when may we expect you back in the fold?"

"On the contrary; I am more than ever determined not to rejoin. Any organisation that prints so much sense from the centre and talks so much drivel around the circumference must be even more rotten than I had supposed."

The report, then, was published in 1938 as a result of sixteen years' work by a commission appointed in 1922 by the then Archbishops of York and Canterbury. It worked under the chairmanship of William Temple, first as Bishop of Manchester and later as Archbishop of York; it included men who were, or subsequently became Bishops of Nottingham, of Chelmsford and of Glasgow, Deans of St. Paul's and of Winchester, Vice-Chancellors of Cambridge and of Manchester Universities and Regius Professor of Divinity at Oxford.

The passages in the report relevant to the present stage in our argument are:

> "The tradition of the inerrancy of the Bible commonly held in the Church until the beginning of the nineteenth century (though often held in association with allegorical interpretations which profoundly modified its significance) cannot be maintained in the light of the knowledge now at our disposal. It will already have become apparent that this belief in its inerrancy is in our judgment in no way necessary

to a full acceptance of the Bible as conveying to us God's revelation of himself." Page 29.

"The authority ascribed to the Bible must not be interpreted as prejudging the conclusions of historical, critical and scientific investigation in any field, not excluding that of the Biblical documents themselves." Page 32.

"No objection to a theory of evolution can be drawn from the two Creation narratives in Gen. i. and ii., since it is generally agreed among educated Christians that these are mythological in origin, and that their value for us is symbolic rather than historical." Page 45.

So much for the old argument about Church and Science. At the centre and at the highest levels of Christian education and authority, it is all over. Nor has it ended in defeat.

It is perfectly true that all leading churchmen have now moved from the positions which some leading churchmen rather naturally took when the argument broke with its fiercest intensity about a hundred years ago. But this is not retreat; it is advance. At the centre the leaders of the Church have advanced to recognise everything that leaders of Science have to say when speaking in their proper fields. All that remains—and it is enough in all conscience—is to win the battle all round the circumference against all the wiles of rationalisation and of the Devil. This means that the children must have it explained to them often, clearly and joyfully, that being a Christian does not involve their believing in all the queer things that would have to be believed if we stuck to the old view about the verbal inspiration of the Bible.

Then what is the teacher to say about miracles?

Irrespective of his own personal views, I am convinced that he owes it to the class as a whole to make sure that they do not leave school without knowing that today two quite different and indeed almost opposite views about miracles are widely held by sincere Christians who are fully accepted members of the Church. In this situation the teacher himself cannot be expected to be neutral; whatever his own view, he should uninhibitedly proclaim it to the class while at the same time making it clear that he fully accepts as fellow Christians all those who hold the other.

On the one hand, then, stands the conventional view that has been held by the majority of professing Christians during such part of the Church's history as is so far known to us. According to this view, the miracles happened—"just like that"; God is all-powerful and reveals his power in mighty works. In the words of Dr. Temple's report:

> "It is felt by many that miracle has special value, in that it is a striking demonstration of the subordination of the natural order to spiritual ends, and affords particular points at which God's activity is manifested with special clarity and directness."

But there is another view. Those who hold it believe that no physical miracle has in fact ever taken place in the whole of man's religious history. Never, that is to say, have vast agglomerations of billions and billions of molecules been caused to break the laws which normally govern their behaviour.

This leaves wide open the absolute certainty that all through history there have been innumerable "miracles" of spiritual insight. It is not inconsistent with the well-authenticated present-day fact that from time to time certain kinds of illnesses are cured through the mediation of some outstanding personality in conditions that cannot be explained in the doctor's textbooks.

This being so, let us be clear (almost by way of digression) that our religious records are bound to contain stories of healing miracles; and that these stories will fall into three categories: Some will be almost exact accounts of what actually happened; others will be exaggerated accounts based nevertheless on a substratum of fact; and others will be wonder tales without any factual reality whatever. It will often be difficult, if not impossible, to assign a particular story with certainty to its appropriate category; and it will not very much matter.

Returning to the main argument, I have been astonished, in personal encounter, to find how many Christians are today semi-privately and almost half-ashamedly holding what I shall call the unconventional view. In discussion following at least one public meeting I have met eager young Christians, won by the power of Christ despite their discomfort about the conventional view of miracle, and rejoicing with outbursts of visible enthusiasm over the information that a newer view is also permissible. And it is. The next words in Dr. Temple's report are:

> "On the other hand it has to be recognised that many others feel it to be more congruous with the wisdom and majesty of God that the regularities, such as men of science observe in nature and call the Laws of Nature, should serve His purpose *without any need for exceptions on the physical plane*" (My italics).

Nor is this to be regarded as a surrender to Science, for the report goes on in the very next line to say:

> "It is important to notice that the motives leading to this view are not exclusively scientific, but that a religious interest is involved."

I have made it abundantly clear already that this is the view I share; and while still fully acknowledging the rights and the sincerity of those who hold the other, I believe there are reasons for supposing that this will be more and more widely held as we find ourselves more confidently advancing into what I have described as the Adolescence of the Christian Church.

Saints, mystics, prophets and psalmists have always known that God himself is the indescribable mystery. But this has not been, in itself, so deeply appreciated by masses. For them it was not difficult, but natural, to believe in hosts of gods and godlings. Living within a community of people thus believing, it did indeed require a "miracle" of spiritual insight to perceive that there were not all these gods, but One God. Yet once this was perceived and proclaimed by missionaries to simple barbarians, there was nothing particularly wonderful about the One God simply considered in Himself. To make Him mysterious, and to surround the very thought of Him with the proper feelings of awe, it was almost necessary to attribute to him a whole series of physical miracles, performed directly or through His chosen servants.

Today it is different. Masses of men and women no longer naturally believe in hosts of gods. In this pragmatic age, as we have seen, we start by believing nothing. God Himself—the eternal Will and Purpose co-ordinating and sustaining all that happens, but yet not specifically associated with any particular assemblage of twirling neutrons, protons and electrons—*this* in itself is the breath-taking mystery. How can he care for me?

> "May so small a creature cry, and be heard by the God who built the atom and flung out the stars? It is a tremendous affirmation. If anyone can make it lightly, he must be innocent,—and therefore, God bless him! Yet it is the affirmation of the Christian religion."[1]

Yes; in these days nothing need be added to God alone to make Him mysterious. And though it will pain sincere Christians who take the other view, I say to them: In our eyes, you cheapen God when you attribute to Him a series of physical conjuring tricks.

Moreover we feel ourselves to be heirs to "these years of amazing research and fearless interrogation" which open to us the possibility of "the nobler, more reasonable, more comprehensive message than ever our fathers knew."[2] Because of this fearless interrogation we now know a good deal about the ways in which written records came into being in olden days. We know that queer wonder tales have an almost irresistible tendency to collect themselves very quickly around the memory of any outstanding man. What about our own King Arthur? What about the Norse Sagas told of those wonderful shadowy figures flickering through the dim mists of the past? There was a time when missionaries could say, in effect:

> "Here is a book which says that men performed miracles and that One performed more wonderful miracles than any other. What, then, were these men? Who is this Man?"

[1] W. R. Maltby, *The Significance of Jesus* (S.C.M.), first edition, p. 56.
[2] See page 30 above.

In olden days millions could give the missionaries their simple, faithful answers without running into collision with anything else in their minds. Today miracles are changing sides! Knowing what we do know now, the miracle stories contained in our Gospels, far from giving them the authentic ring of heavenly truth, tend to remove them from the realm of hard historical fact and to push them back into the dim shadow land where the Norse Sagas come from.

In any case, how does the matter actually come up in the classroom. Here is an extract from one of the tapes recorded by Harold Loukes and his collaborators:

> "*You see the miracles were given us to prove that Jesus Christ was something more than a human being—that he was God. Have you ever considered how all these miracles that no human being could do, like turning water into wine and raising Lazarus from the dead, might have been done to show us in fact that God had come down to earth?*"
>
> "Well, people can write a book saying that so and so did so and so, but that doesn't mean it is true."[1]

Thus, with a single shot, the nineteenth-century teacher is sunk without trace by the twentieth-century child. Moreover it is possible to think that Dr. Temple and his colleagues would have sympathised more with the child than with the teacher. They write:

> "It has to be recognised that legends involving abnormal events have tended to grow very easily in regard to great religious leaders, and that in consequence it is impossible in the present state of knowledge, to make the same evidential use of narratives of miracles in the Gospels which appeared possible in the past."

Nor must anyone be allowed to think even of this as a sad retreat in the face of the loathsome advance of Science. It is not. It is an advance. This is made clear in the very next sentence of the report which reads:

[1] *Teenage Religion*, p. 22. As in the original, the teacher's comments are in italics.

"This is a religious gain, inasmuch as the use of miracles to force belief appears to have been deliberately rejected by our Lord."[1]

The anxiety aroused by the view here offered most often expresses itself in the question: "What is left?" The Church, it is argued, has staunchly believed in the plain factual truth of the miracles for nearly two thousand years; it is bad enough to have atheists and agnostics challenging and denying them; but if alleged Christians join their voices to the denial, where have we any foundation for anything? Surely the whole Faith will collapse like a pack of cards?

An argument is not necessarily wrong merely because it has the same general shape as one that was used over four hundred years ago. Nevertheless, those who ask their agonising "What is left?" should remember that the very same question was raised by those who insisted on the miraculous physical transubstantiation of bread and wine into flesh and blood. The Church had taught this physical miracle for fifteen hundred years; and I believe it is right to say that the passionate hatreds that blazed out of the debate were enflamed by the fear that if this were denied, then the whole Faith would collapse—perhaps like a pack of cards.

But what will be left?

To begin with, once we are no longer plagued with the idea that the Church is insisting that we all believe that all these things happened—happened, that is to say, in the very same sense as it happened that Harold was struck in the eye by an arrow at the Battle of Hastings—we shall then be released to enjoy and relish and use these stories, to our very great advantage, as parables . . . or simply as stories.

But, more important, we shall use our Bibles differently. Where our ancestors in an earlier age found their faith in stories of physical wonder, we shall more probably be directed towards ours by finding "miracles" of spiritual insight.

Let us consider the story of Elijah and the prophets of Baal in I Kings xviii. Baal's side call on their god all day, but he refuses their sacrifice. At the word of Elijah, God at once burns

[1] *Doctrine in the Church of England*, p. 51.

up his proffered bullocks despite their having been three times drenched in water. At this the people slaughter four hundred and fifty of Baal's prophets by the brook Kishon.

I don't believe it. I don't believe that anything even remotely resembling it ever happened in the whole history of Israel. And the position is made much worse, surely, by the statistically impossible *apologia* that Elijah, the canny peasant weather-forecaster, knew for sure that a lightning stroke was bound to fall just there just then. If a man will not square his shoulders and proclaim a miracle worked by God, far better, surely, to join me in regarding this as one of those "legends involving abnormal events" that have "tended to grow very easily in regard to great religious leaders."

Then does this leave our age with vacuum where our ancestors drew inspiration from Elijah? By no means. To begin with, even if it has no shred of factual truth, it is still a gorgeous story. I can relish every moment of it. With the eye of conscious intellect wide open, and with a glimmering of new psychological knowledge about the influence of racial memory, I can "live" in the story and savour all the power by which it has brought to generations of my ancestors some inkling of the wonder and majesty of God. I know that in the very depth of my being I am only variably amenable to pure reason; let me then in part be moulded there by this superb legend.

But there is something more important. That a particular legend has in fact grown around some alleged religious leader, gives us a kind of hunch—(far less than a proof, of course)—that there may have been a pioneer of some kind working at the time and place in question and so providing the peg, as it were, on which the legend has been hung. With this in mind, let us look at Chapter xix of the First Book of Kings. Elijah, discouraged and defeated by the unlimited power of the Baal-worshipping Queen Jezebel—(an utterly incredible situation, surely, for anyone who believes in Chapter xviii and also knows how to put two and two together)—withdraws to a desert cave. He experiences fire, earthquake and tempestuous wind—and it does not matter whether he experiences them in objective fact or in subjective imagination. These, together with lightning flashes, were the outward phenomena in which God's presence was in those days normally discerned. But he sees: God is not in any of these natural wonders; God is in the small still voice that speaks to man. Speaks from inside? Or from outside? Who knows! This is the discovery of a great religious pioneer.

Nor is this all. Elijah is defeated. All the world—all Israel which was for him the world—has gone after Baal and his gluttonous and sexual perversities. Normally in those days men found proof of God's presence in His victory, and in the public discomfiture of His ungodly enemies. But now, in outward failure, Elijah hears the still small voice of God:

> "Yet I have left me seven thousand in Israel, all the knees which have not bowed unto Baal, and every mouth which hath not kissed him."

What an inspiration, stretching across more than two and a half millennia, to reach us here in our wretched twentieth century when everything decent seems to be trampled down under the worship of Mars and Mammon. Seven thousand! Or perhaps, working on about the same proportion in our rather larger population, we may hope there are still a few thousand more who have not bowed the knee to the Get-ahead-Jack philosophy of the age, and have not kissed My-country-right-or-wrong!

I should like to consider the New Testament miracles, and the Resurrection, in the last chapter, but a word must be said here about the Doctrine of the Virgin Birth.

Here perhaps is the elucidation of a minor mystery. I have often asked learned churchmen how to explain the "bushel" that has smothered the bright light of William Temple's great report on doctrine; and have even badgered one or two of the surviving authors for a possible explanation. Usually people have "hummed" and "hawed" and said something about the report coming out at a bad time just before the war, and about its dealing with questions that agitated men's minds in the mid-twenties, and "my dear fellow, you know, these just aren't the same problems as people are interested in today; so although it's good in its way, it has really rather dropped out of date."

Too bad. I suspect that the real reason why it has been smothered is that bishops and clergy have been scared stiff about what might happen if too many churchwardens and organists and, for that matter, too many secondary school boys and school girls, got to know what Temple and his colleagues said about the Virgin Birth.

Temple made his own position clear beyond question in his Chairman's Introduction to the report as a whole.

> "I think it right here to affirm," he said, "that I wholeheartedly accept as historical facts the Birth of our Lord from a Virgin Mother and the Resurrection of His physical body from death and the tomb. And I anticipate, though with less assurance, that these events will appear to be intrinsically bound up with His Deity when the relations between the spiritual and physical elements in our nature are more completely understood."

Does this mean that in Temple's view all who call themselves Christians must accept the same conclusions? It does not. For he goes on:

> "But I fully recognise the position of those who sincerely affirm the reality of our Lord's Incarnation without accepting one or both of these two events as actual historical occurrences, regarding the records rather as parables than as history, a presentation of spiritual truth in narrative form."[1]

The same view stands out from the body of the report. The members of the commission clearly set out the traditional view that has been accepted by the overwhelming majority of professing Christians down the last nineteen hundred years; they summarise the main reasons that have lead most Christians to hold it; they say that "many" (and one has a feeling that this covers an actual majority) of the members of the commission adhere to this long-established faith. They then continue:

[1] *Op. cit.*, p. 12.

> "There are, however, some among us who hold that a full belief in the historical Incarnation is more consistent with the supposition that our Lord's birth took place under the normal conditions of human generation."

So the members of this authoritative commission were "split" on this issue? If anyone wants to put it so; Yes. But they were unanimous in their final judgment.

> "We recognise," they said, speaking as a united body, "that both the views outlined above are held by members of the Church, as of the Commission, who fully accept the reality of our Lord's Incarnation, which is the central truth of the Christian faith."[1]

I have quoted nearly two hundred words from the introduction and the body of the report so as to establish a proposition whose essence can be reduced into eleven: *You can be a Christian without believing in the Virgin Birth.*

I should let the matter rest at that, but for the fact that in public discussion I have been questioned, criticised and even attacked as if I had been saying something far more aggressive. Manifestly I will not repeatedly claim the support of Dr. Temple's writing only to turn round at this point and say that here he must be wrong and I right. Incidentally, medical science has now recorded so many authentic instances of parthogenesis that a belief in the Virgin Birth is not inconsistent with the view that no physical miracle has ever taken place in the whole religious history of man. No: I do not contend that my view must be right; with the backing of Dr. Temple, I ask all Christians to agree that it is permissible.

If this is agreed, an important teaching question remains: Should fifteen-year-olds be allowed to leave school without ever having been told about it? In my view, the Devil is greatly helped by their present state of ignorance. It is such a dead easy rationalisation: "Christians are the sort of people who believe in the Virgin Birth. Rubbish! Christianity's no good to me."

Nor is this crude attitude entirely divorced from more

[1] *Op. cit.*, pp. 82-3.

scholarly support. Many sixth formers get to know that at least from the fourth century B.C. to the second A.D. every little mythological god and godling all round the Mediterranean world had to have some kind of wonder story about his birth. The fact, then, that our Gospels likewise contain a wonder birth story, far from spreading an added sense of holiness over the record of our Lord's life and teaching, merely tilts the whole thing towards the level of ancient mythology. Surely these boys will be helped towards Christianity when they know that belief in the Virgin Birth is not an obligatory part of Christian faith.

And what about Dr. Temple's expectation that more and more of us will share his faith in the Virgin Birth as we better understand our own phsyical and spiritual being? If he is right, will it not be much better that each believer shall come to this part of his belief voluntarily, as a result of a conviction that has come to his own deepest heart, and knowing that he is not in any sense "compelled" or "required" to accept this belief by the Church of which he would call himself a member?

Still concerned with the problem of telling the children what they do not have to start believing, we must briefly notice a tangle of old language, old theories and old analogies that have often done valuable service in a bygone age, but can do deadly damage today. We must remember, once again, that they do their damage through rationalisation. It only needs a distant echo from one of these out-dated notions to drift into an adolescent mind; thereupon the words of the echo, far from receiving the fifteenth-century, or even the third-century connotation that would be given to them automatically by anyone who had spent three or four years at a theological training college, are immediately interpreted according to their literalistic twentieth-century meaning; thus interpreted, they form pictures, or images, in the adolescent's mind. And looking at these pictures, and believing them to be the kind of thing that Christians now believe, it is the likeliest thing in the world that he will slam shut the doors of his mind against the possibility of Christian truth.

All analogies based on animal sacrifice are highly dangerous from this point of view. If he is sure that it can be done without misunderstanding, the teacher may tell the class that even today Christians who are well advanced in their faith may contemplate the Lamb of God slain for the sins of the world; understanding something of Christian history and of men's state of mind in ancient times, they may greatly gain by doing so. But for beginners and for those who have not yet made their first basic religious decision, the teacher should make it clear that this old language is from a dead past; that men of old did indeed try to interpret the mysterious truth in these queer ways; but that in these days we do not. No more than the chemistry master now interprets fire in terms of phlogiston!

The same is true of all the language based on the procedure of the law court. Legalistically-minded Romans may have been helped towards some first flicker of an understanding of all that is meant by the Atonement, when they were offered the analogy of Man in the dock, justly convicted on account of Sin, awaiting sentence from the just Judge, until the innocent Saviour and Advocate stands forth and says: "No; let me suffer instead." Such analogy is in flagrant contradiction to the firmly established morality of the secondary school playground. And we are dealing with secondary school children, not with Roman lawyers. All language deriving from this theory must be excluded from the children's minds by the resolute action of the teacher; because once it gets in, it will start doing the Devil's work as described above.

There must be scores of books giving sympathetic accounts of the old Christian theories which did yeoman service in conveying some part of the ineffable truth to the men of long ago. A short one, including a splendid contemporary interpretation of the Atonement, as well as many footnote references to fuller and more scholarly works, is the book I have quoted already: Leslie Weatherhead's *A Plain Man looks at the Cross*.

What about the Fall of Man?

Now we tread upon difficult ground, for there are many clear-thinking courageous Christians who deeply feel that here we have, not some optional extra, but the very heart and core of the whole Christian teaching about Man. And, what's more, we have here the awful Truth which four hundred years of ever-increasing human "enlightenment" and human arrogance have been cumulatively neglecting, to the present ghastly peril of the whole human race. These Christians will say, further, that nothing—yes, but absolutely nothing—is more uncompromisingly essential for the salvation of mankind (indeed, even for basic survival) than that this crucial neglected Truth should be re-learned by this misguided generation at the earliest possible moment.

Every word of this is correct.

I shall come back to it later in the hope of showing any open-minded adolescent how this hideous state of affairs has been brought about and what it means for his own life in the second half of the twentieth century.

At the moment I am only concerned to argue with educated Christians who understand what has been set out in the preceding paragraphs. These Christians will remember that words and formulae are never sacrosanct, even when they have been venerated for almost seven hundred thousand days. What matters is not words, but Truth. Will these Christians ask themselves, then, in all solemnity, whether we are forwarding Truth on earth by offering it to the uninstructed in language which harks back to this idea about a Fall?

First; are we using the language allegorically?

There is nothing wrong in using allegorical language with secondary modern school children in the Religion and Life Discussion Period, provided we have made certain that they know that it is allegorical language and not to be taken literalistically. Modern psychologists know all about the immense power of allegory—the power of good allegory to do good, and of not-so-good allegory to do harm. Is "The Fall" even a good allegory by which to convey some understanding of man's present state to the children of the twentieth century? Is it true, even allegorically speaking, that we have *fallen down* into our present condition so that, by clear implication, our one great need is to *get back* to where we were before. To speak only to those who are trying to make a really serious study of man's present spiritual predicament, could one read *The Phenomenon of Man*, by Pierre Taillard de Chardin, and then suppose that the situation and its challenge could be wisely pictorialised in terms of a need for turning back? Would any such mental picture of our condition be accepted as creative by the ever-increasing number of psychologists who recognise the imperative need for a religious attitude to life? Are we not much more likely to be creative if we can find some allegory, or paint some picture, which suggests how it is that man has *grown up* into his present state and needs to *go on* and learn more and understand more if he is to see any hope of escape from it?

Consider the interchange between John Freeman and Professor C. G. Jung in "Face to Face" on B.B.C. television in the spring of 1960, (Freeman's contributions in italics):

> "One thing is sure. A great change in our psychological attitude is imminent. That is certain."
>
> "*Now why?*"
>
> "Because we need more—we need more psychology. We need more understanding of human nature, because the only real danger that exists is man himself. He is the great danger, and we are pitifully unaware of it. We know nothing of man, far too little. His psyche should be studied, because we are the origin of all coming evil."
>
> "*Well, does man, do you think, need to have the concept of sin and evil to live with? Is this part of his nature?*"
>
> "Well, obviously."
>
> "*And of a personal redeemer?*"
>
> "That is an inevitable consequence."

Does not this language of Jung's suggest the need for going forward to a level of understanding that man has never previously known? And is it not therefore unwise, to say the least, if we put into the minds of children something so vastly potent as an allegory which suggests that our problem is that of finding the way back to where we were before? Potentially the modern psychologists are amongst our strongest allies. But if our Christian allegories portray man's religious task in terms of climbing back, the Devil and the powers of rationalisation might easily turn them into our enemies.

There are Christian propagandists, including some who have won great influence, who use words that can have no other effect than to suggest that the Fall is not a mere allegory, but an historic event, whose exact date we do not know, but whose occurrence is of the same order of historicity as are, say, the early Egyptian dynasties. This language does not suggest that early men, slowly evolving the attributes of human self-consciousness and human personality, correspondingly evolved over thousands of years the ability to make choice between good and evil . . . and often chose evil. The language used by these Christians is quite meaningless unless they wish us to understand that there was an actual time when men, women and children, with all the attributes of full self-consciousness and personality, chose to live in glorious, blameless harmony with each other and the Lord; and that from this heaven-on-earth they Fell.

One must be perfectly blunt. This kind of language, offered to the children of the twentieth century, is meaningless. Those who offer it do the Devil's work for him. No archaeologist, no anthropologist, nor any other investigator or thinker approaching the problem of man in a scientific temper has ever found in the whole human record any shadow of a trace of this perfect heavenly state from which, it is alleged, men fell away at some definite though unknown date. There is nothing in the whole "tree" of evolution which suggests that anything like it ever occurred, or ever could have occurred. And if we put into children's minds vague and powerful pictures that are clean contrary to everything that science has to say about us, then the Devil will know how to make use of them to exclude the Christian Truth.

And why? Why, why, why should these Christians insist on this queer antiquarianism when, as we shall see later, every single thing that the men of old time understood as Original Sin may now be explained, reinforced and hammered home in terms which are at all points in line with everything that the scientific psychologists are now beginning to find out about us?

Whatever anyone else may think of all this, I am glad to find that here as elsewhere my views are merely an echo of those of Dr. Temple and his colleagues who wrote *Doctrine in th Church of England*. They state their conclusion very clearly:

> "In our view the doctrine of a universal tendency to ev in man is not bound up with the historical truth of any stor of a Fall."[1]

A FOOTNOTE ON PERSONAL HONESTY

I must add here a note on detail as otherwise I shall be con victed of dishonesty by anyone who troubles to look up Harol Loukes's *Teenage Religion* at page 22. I have omitted a significan contribution from one of the children. Between the teacher claim for miraculous authority and the child's devastatin reply, another child speaks up on the teacher's side. She say of the miracles:

"Well, that's why he did the miracles—to show people tha he was God."

Now that the omission has been disclosed it may be aske why one should neglect the faithful little child and acclaim th beastly cynic? And, more important, why risk shattering th simple faith of the one for the brash unbelief of the other?

One answer is that the child whom we now rather unfairl call the cynic has learned what the school and the twentiet century are teaching about not believing all we see in print and the other child has not.

But a more important point arises. It would be wrong to b dogmatic about it; but are we once again in the presence of rationalisation? What I mean is that no one would like t confront himself and say outright: "I shall stick to the dear ol ways of teaching because I am too lazy and timid to tr anything new." So much better if he can say to himself: "C course I'd be glad to try anything that would really help but one must not disturb the simple faith of one of these simpl souls, now, must one?"

If it is put like this, there are two answers. Firstly, suppos that the teacher (who is, after all, a Christian) does not take th trouble to introduce the simple soul sympathetically to th thought and challenge of the twentieth century, what is goin

[1] *Op. cit.*, p. 69.

to happen to the simple faith when the child meets a really professional cynic, say, at the age of seventeen?

The second answer is perhaps more difficult to grasp. It depends on the difference between things seen because they do happen, and things not seen because they do not happen but might have happened. One of the largest world-scale examples of this kind of thing is that many are apt to see the numbers—the appalling numbers—who were killed in communal rioting when self-government was given to India and Pakistan. They are apt not to see the greater numbers who would have lost their lives by now if serious postponement of self-government had reduced the whole Indian sub-continent to the state of what was then called French Indo-China.

In the same way, we see the "simple souls"; they come to church (at any rate up to the age of about seventeen); and we assume (or is it that the Devil wants us to assume?) that their faith would have died of indigestion if we had offered them the strong meat of a more up-to-date message. But even if that assumption were true (which it is not), it still takes no account of the larger numbers whom we do not see. We do not see them because they do not come to church; and they do not come because the poor, thin diet we serve up for the sake of the simple souls, leaves them starved of the contemporary spiritual nourishment that they need.

CHAPTER SEVEN

COPING WITH "PROVE IT!"

We have said that the essential fact in our new egalitarian age is not that we are all equal. The essence of our new way of life is that each in accordance with his own abilities and limitations, shall be privileged and burdened with the task of making his own decision on fundamentals. Wiser and older men and women, on behalf of the whole community, may guide and advise the younger. But in the end, everybody makes his own choice.

> "Basic to all modern teaching is the modern empirical standpoint that says: 'Don't believe everything that anyone tells you; examine the evidence; look at the facts.' Such a standpoint is the great safeguard of the free way of life, particularly against fanatical ideologies."[1]

So the adolescent is to make up his own mind?

How?

When he is offered some important proposition to accept and believe, how does he start to tackle it? As naturally as the mole to the earth or the buzzard to the air, he will tackle the proposition with "Prove it!" And this is because he lives in a science-minded age.

He is not himself a scientist. Incidentally, if he were a really modern scientist our R.E. problem would be three-quarters solved for us. But no; he is a technologist and the son of a technologist. Misunderstanding and possible criticism might have been avoided if our times had been described from the start as the opening decades of the "technology-minded" age. But the phrase was too clumsy. And in any case, the technologists derive from the scientists. Their ways of thought, with many

[1] P. W. Martin, in *Education for Teaching*, November 1959.

of the refinements missing and with the sharp edge of accuracy blunted, are ultimately of the same order as the scientists'. For three hundred years and more, with dazzling results, the scientists have been straining forward and outward to look at the world—to look with ever increasing accuracy at everything that the technologist would call (but the scientist would not now call) the solid material world all round us. From this world the scientist draws his evidence; to the evidence he applies his logic. For scientist:

Evidence + Logic = Truth

For technologist:

Evidence + Logic + Practical Application = Prosperity

Little wonder, then, if the shape of our thinking has been transformed by all the wonders that have burst upon us in the last few generations; little wonder if we are concerned—or as some might say, obsessed—by this question of "proof" in the sense in which the word is used by our technological generation. Let us look at another of the live discussions that have been recorded for us through one of Harold Loukes's tape recorders. As in the original, the teacher's contributions are in italics.

"In Maths and Science today we don't accept anything until it's proved—we say well if x equals so and so, then the so and so must equal x, and we don't accept anything until it is proved.'

"*How can you prove that the sunset is beautiful by* x*? How can you prove your mother's love?*"

"You can't."

"Well, love isn't like that—you feel love, you can't just say that love is over there."

"*What I mean is, there is more than one way of proving something. You can do it in a mathematical way, or you can do it by using your imagination with the sunset, or again with the love of your mother.*"

"Yes, but it was all such a long time ago. If I hear

something I like to have it proved, and that's why I don't go to Church or anything like that."

"So what sort of proof are you wanting? You see there is emphatic proof, and scientific proof, and all sorts of proof. That's what I am getting at. I want to know how you can explain the Christian Church 2,000 years later if Jesus never lived?"[1]

If I were offering this material in a college lecture, instead of in a book for general publication, I should break off at this point and send the students away for a week to write critical essays on this interchange. Any teacher, or intending teacher, may care to jot down the headings of some of the paragraphs that he would include in such an essay. Because, without wishing to withold the due measure of praise from the spirited quality of the teacher's contribution, it is possible to feel that she has fallen into a network of error so complex as to need a good deal of disentanglement.

To begin with, one wonders whether her last four words were so spoken and emphasised as to convey to the class an accurate impression of what may be understood from their meticulous examination when we see them written down? If they were, then the teacher was inviting the children to confront an issue of no real importance. Neither we, nor the agnostics, are controversially involved over the mere question whether Jesus lived. Almost every Humanist, looking at ascertainable Church history and at the verifiable Christian documents, will agree to a proposition so flat and unmoving as that someone known as Jesus lived at or about the time and place alleged and did something or other that caused his followers to write the documents and start the movement that we know. So what?

The real controversy is something quite other. And one can hardly doubt that the teacher intended to refer, and that the class took her to be referring, to this real and living issue. Though the last words were unspoken, there was, surely, an unmistakable addition to her question: "I want to know how

[1] *Teenage Religion*, pp. 22-3. In case I am suspected of anti-feminism in what follows, I should perhaps say that it is clear from other evidence that all who take part in this discussion are female.

you can explain the Christian Church 2,000 years later if Jesus never lived *and if the Christian claims about him are not true*?" And though it is unfair to pass final judgment without hearing the teacher's tone of voice, yet there does not seem to be much point in the question unless it is asked in a way that implies that you cannot do it.

Now it may very well be that there was no child in the teacher's class—perhaps no child in the school—who could sit down and write an essay to show how the Christian Church might have grown, and might have persisted as it has, even though Jesus were not "the Son of God". But there are men and women in our country who could; and the teacher well knows it!

What about Sir Julian Huxley and all the other contributors to his recent *Humanist Frame*? Can it be disputed that they are all serious and dedicated servants of beauty, love and truth? Does the teacher seriously suppose that they have reached their present position, and built up the whole philosophy on which they are now living, without considering and without answering, to their own sincere satisfaction, this argument of hers: That the mere existence of the organised Church through 2,000 years *proves* the divinity of Jesus? Or does she hope that the children in her class will never hear of this company of men and women? Or that they will never read their serious arguments?

Well, perhaps those children never will read such arguments. But does the teacher suppose that they will go through life—or even through the next five years—without being brought up against some echo, or some garbled or sloganised version, of the argument by which Humanists could perfectly well explain the whole chequered history of the Church without having to grant anything special about Jesus?

And if some of the children leave school with the impression —which, surely, the teacher intended—that somehow Church history proves Christ's divinity, what are they expected to do when they meet these echoes and garbled slogans? Will they argue back? If so, where will the argument lead? The Devil will have to be very unlucky if it is not to lead to the position of a student at a teacher training college who lamented:

> "If only we could have got down to basic principles more, we might now be able to argue with agnostics and atheists instead of all being bested in argument and our faith laughed at."[1]

But let us come a little nearer to the general problem of Proof. The teacher on the tape tells us that there are different sorts of proof. "There is emphatic proof, and scientific proof and there is more than one way of proving something; you can do it in a mathematical way, or you can do it by using your imagination."

Of course there are various kinds of proof. But is our teacher justified in implying that they are so very varied as to allow her to suggest that you can "do it" by using your imagination? So as to ward off possible criticism, it would be as well to say that at a later stage I shall argue that one can do many things by a process not very different from using your imagination. But at this point I am only concerned to ask whether it is wise, or even really honest, to mix all this up with the question of proof.

It may be suggested that "it all depends" on what you mean by proof. But teachers have almost no personal liberty in the meanings which they give to words. The teacher whom I am criticising is not entitled to say that the criticism must be rejected as soon as we give to "proof" the meaning that she intended to convey. For teachers—particularly in Secondary Schools—there is only one test of meaning: "What do the children of this technological age mean by the word when they use it in conversation with each other?" I think it is dishonest, and I am sure it is like bashing one's head against a wall, to use a word in an R.E. lesson in any other sense.

Then what do we mean by "proof"?

As has been said, there are several kinds. There is the mathematician's proof, which is the most absolute of all. It proceeds

[1] Dr. J. W. Daines, *Enquiry into Religious Education* (Nottingham Institute of Education), p. 23.

from accurately defined concepts, through unchallengeable logic, to inescapable conclusions. The physicist's proof is not quite so certain because observation is involved as well as logic. And so, for example, although for all practical purposes light travels in straight lines, as was proved by physicists long ago, yet we may now learn that at the speeds involved in outer space and in the heart of the atom, the solid proof of yesterday has been upset by the observations and logic of today. The lawyer's proof is even less reliable, as we know from such rare horrors as the Timothy Evans verdict. Nevertheless, in ordinary life, when witnesses assemble and evidence piles up, we say quite correctly that a point comes when the thing has been proved. The historian's proof and the archaeologist's proof are of the same kind except that the witnesses, instead of living men and women, are original documents from the archives, or bones from ancient strata tested perhaps for age by the radio-carbon technique.

Looking at these different kinds of proof, and extracting from them what they have in common, what do we take to be the meaning of the word?

A proof is a process compounded of observation and logic at the end of which, for all practical purposes, the mind of the technologist is compelled to give assent to the proposition in question. No; not *the* mind of *the* technologist. If the proof is really a proof, then all the minds of all the technologists in the world will be compelled to give assent, provided only that their I.Q. is high enough to enable them to follow the argument.

So what shall we do?

Shall we reluctantly admit that our alleged proofs, though highly suggestive, are not quite conclusive? Surely not. Anything that is to be learned needs to be offered with joy and zest —two qualities that are markedly absent from reluctant admissions. Whatever is to be done, it must be proclaimed!

When I was about fifteen I looked at the historic Christian proofs of God and found that every one of them could be shot to ribbons by agnostic cross-examination. I therefore concluded that God cannot exist; "because", said I, "if He does exist, you Christians ought to be able to prove it; and you can't;

therefore He doesn't; Q.E.D." I was bogged down at this boundary between agnosticism and atheism for years on end until Dr. James Parkes, in his Penguin book *Good God*, came along and told me:

> "God intends you to be free; free above all else to believe in Him, or not. A proof is a process that compels assent. Therefore, not through the weakness of Christians, but by the grace of God, there is never never never going to be any proof of His existence."[1]

Of course Parkes did not *compel* me to believe; but for the first time in years he laid my mind open and *allowed* me to believe; whereas previously I had been forbidden to believe by my misunderstanding of the relation between God and Proof.

Of course all this opens up the possibility that the teacher may find himself challenged by the bright child who says that in the old days Christians thought they could prove God; and if teacher now says we cannot, doesn't this show that Christians are all wrong anyway.

This, if it arises, is but a particular example of the widespread belief that the religious vision is not allowed to expand and grow; and it must be treated as such. It is to be hoped that the teacher will still have on the wall the time chart that we mentioned in Chapter Six. If so, he can easily point out that "in that age" they do indeed seem to have believed that God's existence could be proved by logical argument. Earlier still they believed that whole tribes could and should be compelled to believe by threat of fire and sword. We must not entirely condemn them. By our standards and, we may surely say, by absolute standards as well, they were ignorant and foolish in the one case and wicked in the other. But their queer beliefs and nasty practices sprang in part out of their rock-solid faith in God, and out of the feeling (correct in itself) that by comparison nothing else on earth mattered in the least. But man's religious perception grows and clarifies. Whatever they may have thought in any other age, in this age we know that we are not

[1] This is not a quotation; it is a summary of the effect Parkes had on me. The book was written under his pen name, John Hadham.

allowed to convert whole tribes by fire and slaughter, and cannot convert whole housing estates, nor even one single solitary human soul, by pretending to have a proof.

Some time shortly before the end of his last term with any class, particularly if the majority of the pupils will then be leaving school, the teacher ought to take a solemn opportunity of working out the implications of all this on arguments between Christians and their opponents. It may very well be that in these days this kind of argument is not very frequent, partly because the opponent does not think it worth bothering, and partly because the Christian, like the teacher trainee, fears we will be "bested in argument and our faith laughed at". This is very largely due to the fact that the Christian, because he "did not get down to basic principles more", too often allows his opponent, and any audience that may be listening, to start the whole thing on the wrong footing. Too often Christian and opponent and audience start (as I did at fifteen) with the assumption that the Christian has to prove something; and the assumption will be all the firmer for being unspoken and usually no more than semi-conscious. So the Christian sets off accordingly. The opponent choses his point of attack wherever the Christian seems weakest. The Christian volubly reinforces his argument at the point where it is criticised, only to find that the opponent has nimbly jumped on to some other ground and is making mincemeat of his proof from some different direction. And the audience laughs.

This will never do. It will always fail, and fail deservedly, because it started wrong.

If any Christian should find himself deliberately or casually invited into an argument about Christianity in front of many or in front of few, he should never advance a step into it until he is absolutely confident that opponent and audience have clearly understood what James Parkes told me in his book *Good God*. As soon as this has been understood, then, with any luck, the Christian can go over to the counter-attack, with:

> "This fellow here is trying to tell us there isn't such a thing as God. He makes out that the whole show can be explained

> mechanically and that the scientists understand it all. Right; I challenge him: Take a simple proposition; take '*I see a red pillar-box*', and go ahead and show us how a simple little job like that can work itself mechanically."

Of course the opponent may be wise enough to avoid the challenge, in which case the audience may take the point when it is suggested that if he won't even undertake to prove a godless pillar-box, he'd better start being a little less cocksure about godless Life.

But given only the normal amount of luck, the opponent will wade in. Unfortunately it may take quite a time. He will speak of rays of light—white light compounded of different wave-lengths—pigments in paint are chemically such as to absorb some wave-lengths and reflect others—thence to refraction of light rays as they pass from rarer to denser media—so to lenses and their action in focusing images of illuminated objects on to the retina of eyeballs—thence to photosensitive cells which translate light waves of differing frequencies into minute electric currents minutely varying in strength with a periodicity that corresponds with the wave-length of the light that falls on the cell. In the end we shall arrive at something like this:

(An electric current
varying in a nerve with
relatively *low* periodicity) = (I see *red*)

and

(An electric current
varying in a nerve with
relatively *high* periodicity) = (I see *violet*)

Splendid! But what on earth are those "equals" doing? Might one not just as well say that autumn leaves, when falling on the lawn at a low rate, are equal to five hundred pounds in the bank; and when falling at a rapid rate are equal to six hundred. If anyone says that there is no connection between autumn leaves and money in the bank, then, *in exactly the same way*, there is no logical connection whatsoever between an electric current varying with a given periodicity and "I see red".

At this point the opponent may ask whether the Christian is trying to insinuate that it must be God miraculously turning current into sight. But no; the Christian must revert to the starting-point; he is not trying to *prove* anything. God intends even the atheist opponent to be free to believe or not; and therefore there is never going to be a proof. The only suggestion is that if people cannot even explain how we see a letterbox on scientific principles, they might think again before feeling sure that they can run the whole of Life without God.

At this point, if there is an audience, someone may ask how it happens that Christians go around talking so confidently of something that cannot be proved. It may suffice, at the end of a strenuous argument, for the Christian to come back with a question of his own:

> "Do you suppose that in the whole mysterious business of Life there is no knowledge of anything except through the rigid processes that scientists, mathematicians and lawyers call 'Proof'?"

This, however, will hardly serve as the long-term answer for the teacher who may be asked the same kind of question in the classroom. He may face a real problem; for it may be that, at the stage then reached, there will be the gravest difficulty about accepting the only real answers. Happy the teacher who meets his class at the beginning of their third year with good hope of keeping them through to the end of their fourth. He may properly ask his questioners to take an alert interest in the Religion and Life Discussion Periods for the next four or five terms and see whether they do not find the answers for themselves.

I face a rather similar difficulty at this stage with that almost mythical figure—the average reader. There are whole realms of knowledge, and particularly of self-knowledge, that may be necessary for anything like a fully acceptable answer to the question; and these may be almost unknown to an "average reader" for no other reason than that no teacher has ever bothered to tell him about them in the idiom of our twentieth century.

May I then offer this reader the same kind of answer as the fortunate teacher might give to his class? Will he stay with me for another three chapters and see if acceptable answers then begin to emerge?

CHAPTER EIGHT

WHERE IS THE POSITIVE STARTING-POINT?

WE HAVE CONSIDERED only two aspects of the recent change in man's basic thought-patterns: from authoritarian to egalitarian, and from pre-scientific to scientific. This has lead us to two negative conclusions: We must make sure that adolescents know that they are not expected to believe the impossible; we must make sure that they are not expecting a proof in the ordinary meaning of the word. These conclusions, though necessary, will remain useless unless they can be co-ordinated into something positive.

In the hope of finding it, may we summarise the other aspects of the great change in outlook that still remain to be taken into account.

The men, women and adolescents of a bygone age had not isolated Reason from the other human faculties. They made their judgments—(their childish judgments, if anyone wants to say so)—with the Whole Being. They had a vivid sense of sin; crudely, perhaps, but very definitely they acknowledged their own inadequacy. More important still, they were tempermentally much closer to the animal herd than we; they were more firmly integrated with each other, with their own little communities, and hence with Life as a whole. In all these ways they had a fundamentally religious outlook on life that we have not. We saw that they did not know they had it; they simply had it in the sense that they could not have conceived any state of being in which one did not have it.

Our primary school children still live in a somewhat similar state of being.

But we and our adolescent children are different. We live in a society—indeed we constitute a society—"which has

virtually cut itself off from religion". By nature, we do not hav
any such thing as a religious attitude to life. Failing carefu
instruction, we probably live our adult lives without formin
even the vaguest idea about what such an attitude migh
involve.

Taking a long view, the situation is challenging rathe
than depressing. When we know rather more about the necessary teaching methods, we may hope that there will be new generations who will again have a basically religious attitude t
life. But the wonderful thing will be that those generation
will have it consciously, in the sense that the state of being i
which one might not have it will be known to them by livin
experience. Like everything else that we have been discussing
this will constitute a dramatic religious advance on anythin
that has ever been before.

But we must return to the "vast desert which the Church i
traversing today".[1]

If the Bible is put into the hands of people who are basicall
religious—(be they the adults of an earlier day or the littl
children of our own)—it can work its inspiration straigh
away. Particularly if they are guided to the most glorious passages, they feel that they know what it is about; it is in harmon
with their own ideas and emotions; it speaks to their conditio
and their need.

But what happens if we put the Bible to people who ar
basically non-religious, irreligious, a-religious—call them whic
you will? There they sit, the serried ranks of teenagers in ou
Secondary Schools; and without giving them any idea abou
what is involved in the religious attitude as such, we are solemnl
advised in every Agreed Syllabus drawn up by every L.E.A.
in the country to take them through the journeys of Paul, th
vision of Ezekiel, the Synoptic Problem, the social state o
Judah on the brink of the captivity, the history of the earl
Church, the aspirations of Nehemiah on the return—and, o
course, the Gospels themselves. True enough, of course, tha
within all this—and particularly within the Gospels—here and

[1] See again the quotation from Frederick Stokes just after the title page of thi
book.

there a wonderful sentence of pure inspiration, or a glorious passage of religious poetry, will carry its challenge or its peace into the heart of one of our teenagers despite all the "armour plating" that our godless society has bent around them. And so, someone may think, our teaching will at least do just a little good.

But no! *On balance* the work we are doing now in Secondary Schools probably does harm. In this sense Arthur Barton was right in saying that

> "it would do religion no harm, and perhaps a great deal of good, if it could be cut right out of the State school curriculum, at any rate after the primary stage."[1]

If we simply left the teenagers alone, their own need and the Holy Spirit might lead a good many of them towards the Truth. By pushing the Bible at them when, for want of a basically religious outlook, they cannot understand its message, we are in most cases strengthening the armour plating that stands between them and God. We send them out of our schools saying—or, far more deadly, merely feeling without ever putting sharp words on to their frustration:

> "If *that* was religion . . . and teacher 'said' it was . . . and teacher ought to know . . . but if that *was* religion, then religion has no use for me and no relevance to my Life."

We are being led to what many will feel to be an astonishing—even an appalling—conclusion: Once the innocent primary stage is over in this second half of our twentieth century, the approach to religion in general and to Christianity in particular does not start from the Bible; does not start from God; does not even start from Christ.

If this seems surprising, let us check it. We want teenagers to learn to read the Bible with appreciation. We want them to realise the truth about God as revealed in Jesus Christ. These are the conclusions that we hope they will reach—or, to speak with greater theological accuracy, that we hope will reach them—as a consequence of our teaching. Is there any other

[1] See my slightly garbled quotation from his article on page 15 above.

subject in the twentieth-century curriculum in which it could seem sensible to *start* at the *conclusion*? Surely not; for if there is a theme which I have heard continually from my superiors in a teacher training college it is:

> Start from the known and work to the unknown; start from where the children are; start with their actual ideas, their actual knowledge, their actual feelings and their actual interests; and from these, help the children to go forward to whatever-it-is that needs to be known."

With this in mind, are we very shocked by Paul Tillich who writes:

> "It cannot be required of the man of today that he first accept theological truths, even though they should be God and Christ. Wherever the Church in its message makes this a primary demand, it does not take seriously the situation of the man of today and has no effective defence against the challenge of many thoughtful men of our day who reject the message of the Church as of no concern for them. The modern man might well say to the Church, using her own language: 'God does not demand that man, in order to experience the unconditioned judgment, the "No" and the "Yes" from above himself, shall first accept a religious tenet about God or shall overcome all doubt concerning him'."[1]

I quoted these words from Tillich in other writing some four or five years ago because I felt their truth, and despite the fact that at the time I should have been hard put to it to find an answer to the obvious question:

> "If God and Christ are not the proper starting-points for religious teaching in Secondary Schools, then where, in heaven or earth, may the proper starting-points be found?"

Today I feel more ready to offer an answer. After all, what is religion? I do not here ask what is Christianity? Christianity

[1] *The Protestant Era* (Nisbet), p. 201.

is one of the great religions which, we believe, holds the Truth in ways that the others do not because of its recognition of the unique initiative of God in Jesus Christ. But what is religion as such? It is not a store of information or knowledge. It is not a set of intellectual abilities. Religion is a relationship. It is not a speculation or a theory about a relationship. A man's religion *is* the relationship between himself and all the other people, the entire community, the whole of Life and whatever beings or Beings may stand behind Life's outward show. More shortly: Religion is the relationship between Oneself and Life.

If, then, we live in an age which has virtually cut itself off from religion—an age in which the great majority of men, women and adolescents have so little appreciation of what is meant by a religious attitude to life that it is useless, and even harmful, to start by putting to them the Bible, God and Christ—this is probably because they know too little about Themselves and too little about Life in the actual world of here and now. Our conclusion, then, is staring us in the face.

The starting-point for religious teaching is in the adolescents themselves.

The starting-point for religious teaching is in the Life of the second half of the twentieth century.

This is the conclusion of my book in the sense that I began to write it for the over-riding purpose of reaching this central point. It is far from being original. Indeed it may well turn out to be the focal point to which many who are seriously concerned with religious teaching are now converging. D. S. Wright of the Department of Psychology in Leicester University writes:

> ". . . we must base the course upon the nature of adolescence, and the nature of the society in which the adolescents are growing up . . . We must take as our starting-point, not a body of knowledge, but the particular adolescents in front of us, and the universe they inhabit. . . .
>
> "The position taken in this paper is that we need to explore

seriously the possibility of a child-centred course in religious instruction."[1]

Let it at least be clear that if we went no further than the point reached by Wright, we should already have substantiated the plea for a revolution in our teaching methods. For textbooks on religious education—be they slender pamphlets to be handed out to every member of the class or massive commentaries for the teachers' shelves—are almost all based on the assumption that the first, and indeed the only, job to be done is to offer the Bible, God and Christ to the teenagers in the Secondary Schools. Many of these textbooks are brilliantly written by men and women fully attuned to the whole spirit of our age and taking full account of all our most contemporary knowledge. But if the job they tell us about is the wrong job, then it will be no use to learn how to do it in a twentieth-century, instead of in a nineteenth-century, idiom.

We need something more.

Indeed if any teacher has followed the argument with agreement, it will be all too obvious to him what he wants next. He wants a complete set of lesson notes showing him how to translate his agreement in principle into detailed weekly classroom practice. I sympathise. But is it reasonable to suppose that anything so problem-free could be handed out at this stage by a single author—by a single teacher? Textbooks, teachers' commentaries and detailed lesson notes arise from a mass of experience which is itself built up out of many years of experimental classroom work undertaken by large numbers of teachers. And even though the conclusion just stated is the very one to which many serious educationists may now be converging, yet we have today hardly begun the experimental work that needs to be based upon it. Wright's judgment seems to be correct: The possibility of a child-centred course needs to be seriously explored.

The rest of this book, then, is an attempt to make just such an exploration—to offer a preliminary survey of some of the territory that might be covered in such a course. For the most part

[1] *A Study of Religious Belief in Sixth Form Boys* (University of Leeds Institute of Education), pp. 2 and 8.

the exploration will be conducted in language well "above" what might actually be offered to third and fourth formers; though occasionally, when trivial experience justifies, we may "descend" to actual phrases, and even to actual diagrams, that might be used in class.

CHAPTER NINE

WHAT ABOUT THE CHILDREN?

IF THE TEACHER'S short-term wish for lesson notes has to be temporarily disappointed, let him take heart when he looks towards the medium-term future. The present task may look difficult; but beyond it the prospects are most encouraging.

What I have in mind is that some adolescents are interested in fishing, and many in cycling. It is always, therefore, a fairly good gimmick to open any lesson with some reference to a bicycle or a fish. The only trouble is that other members of the class may not be quite so keen on either of these occupations. There are only two things in which all adolescents are bound to be interested: One is Themselves; the other is Life in the world of the twentieth century. When it becomes clear that the purpose of discussion periods is to try to know more about these two, and the relationship between them, there is good hope that what were once called the "R.E. Lessons", instead of being the most despised, will become the most respected and most eagerly anticipated events in the school week. There is even a chance that a spirit of impending maturity, emanating from the Religion and Life Discussion Periods, will begin to pervade the whole of the adolescents' last couple of years at school.

At this point in my argument I am led to revise a judgment offered in Chapter Three: At any rate in and above the fourth form this work will need three or four periods in the week.

If the teenagers are to learn a little more about themselves, this is bound to mean, in the second half of the twentieth century, that they must somehow be brought in contact with some of the basic findings of modern psychology.

The teacher may complain that he is not a psychologist. Nor am I. Nevertheless I can assure him of the childrens' attention. Yes; boys who were so indisciplined as to make the classes little short of chaotic when I tried to teach them mathematics, froze into wrapt attention and disciplined questioning whenever one of them succeeded in getting me to talk about psychology instead. Someone may misquote that piece about a little knowledge being dangerous. Maybe; but on this subject it is probably less dangerous than a lot of ignorance.

After all, it is not like physics. A teacher might be justly nervous about teaching physics if he did not know very much about it; because in physics, we are really trying to teach just exactly what physics is; and until we reach university standard, we are teaching what all the physicists in the world agree about. The same is not true about psychology because the psychologists themselves are not agreed, and there is therefore no question of our having to teach the children exactly what it is. The aim, luckily, can be more indefinite. Even if some of the things we say would earn nought out of a hundred in the psychologists' passing out examination, still little harm will have been done and great good may spread, if the adolescents come to the end of their school days with some kind of idea that perhaps this strange creature known as Twentieth-Century Man is more complicated and less self-adequate than is usually supposed.

The contemporary popular idea, steadily developed from the seventeenth to the nineteenth century, is that man is a reasonable creature who ought to be able to rule his life successfully by the exercise of the conscious power of human thought. It is only, of course, in fairly recent times that this notion, with its long historical development behind it, has burst through the surface and come out to dominate our thinking and arguing and planning on all individual and social questions, and to determine so very largely the whole tone and quality of the atmosphere we breathe. It dominates, still, the atmosphere engulfing the vast majority, even though pioneering minorities have long since recognised its absurd inadequacy. Beatrice Webb writes of it:

"Looking back, it now seems to me that it was exactly in those last decades of the nineteenth century that we find the watershed between the metaphysic of the Christian Church, which had hitherto dominated British civilisation, and the agnosticism, deeply coloured by scientific materialism, which was destined, during the first decades of the twentieth century, to submerge all religion based on tradition and revelation."

And later, in referring to the climate of opinion within which she made her own early repudiation of Christianity, she describes the impact of the late-nineteenth-century discovery of Eastern religions, and continues:

> "More widely and deeply influential, because it was associated with the great discoveries of mid-Victorian science, and was, moreover, closely connected with the conduct of affairs, was the then-called 'religion of science': that is, an implicit faith that by the methods of physical science, and by these methods alone, could be solved all the problems arising out of the relation of man to man and of man towards the universe."[1]

Let us see what this means. All problems of human relations are to be solved by the unemotional, uninvolved observation of objectively verifiable facts; and by applying cool, logical argument—the power of human Reason—to the data thus observed and verified. This process, it is thought, will give us all the answers we need because man is taken to be a basically reasonable animal—a creature, that is to say, whose decisions and conduct are effectively governable through knowledge and reason.

If this is true, what follows?

A man reaches certain conclusions. He believes they are correct because he has reached them, as he supposes, through this uninvolved scientific process. But someone disagrees with him. Someone even opposes him. What sort of creature can this be? If he were reasonable, as he should be, he would agree with the conclusion. There must be something wrong with him. Indeed the only possible explanation is that he is somehow less than a normal man; he must be moved by some kind of evil or malevolence.

[1] *My Apprenticeship* (Longmans), pp. 54 and 83.

It may be that our democratic training will restrain some of us from reaching the logical conclusion of this process. But "logically" it leads to the view that these opponents who disagree cannot be real human beings at all. Such distorted creatures should really be liquidated. Hence, in the Albert Hall on November 12th, 1962, when Canon Carpenter was seriously discussing the historic Christian doctrine about the Just War, a member of the audience screamed out at him: "*Any* war against the Communists is a just war!" And at a more elevated level, an example of the earlier stages of the same process is afforded by Bertrand Russell, perhaps the high priest and certainly the father figure of the contemporary rationalist movement. From the prison to which he had heroically chosen to go in pursuit of his beliefs, he said:

> "Kruschev and Kennedy, Adenauer and De Gaulle, Macmillan and Gaitskell are pursuing a common aim, the ending of human rights. You, your families, your friends, and your countries are to be exterminated by the common decision of a few brutal but powerful men. To please these men . . . all that has been achieved . . . is to be wiped out."[1]

To help the teenagers towards a better understanding of themselves and of those who disagree with them, and towards a more religious outlook on life, the teacher might ask them to write down what they understand by "Original Sin".

I have not done it often enough to have evidence which is even modestly statistical. But trivial experience supports the *a priori* supposition that in many answers the teacher would be told about Adam and Eve, and about Eve's disobedience to God, so that somehow some taint of Sin is supposed to have been passed down to all of us by inheritance from the original pair; and that anyway, everyone knows today that the whole thing is nonsense. I have only the very slenderest evidence to support a further hunch: That although nothing would emerge in word or writing unless the teacher-class relationship were exceptionally favourable, yet there would be somewhere in the back of the children's minds some tangled connection between

[1] The *Guardian*, September 1961.

Original Sin and the smouldering fear that somehow, even between husband and wife, there is something shameful about sexual intercourse.

If I have correctly estimated the general tenor of the majority of written answers to the teacher's question, then he will have to begin by ramming it home all over again that there is no historic truth in the story of Adam and Eve and that therefore any idea about our all catching some guilty taint from a single original pair is simply out of the question. He will go on to say, however, that in the mythical story of the Garden of Eden, the visionaries and writers of old time have given us an allegory which pictorialises for us deep truth about the nature of man. The class may even pause a moment and reflect: By Whom were these men inspired when they told and wrote down such a parable containing symbolically so much of the Truth. Just in case anyone should still suppose that Original Sin refers to some past inheritance rather than to a present fact, let me once more turn to the authority of Dr. Temple:

> "The Doctrine of Original Sin," he wrote, "has often been put forward in ways which men today find peculiar difficulty in accepting. . . . Enough for our present purpose may be expressed as follows. When we open our eyes as babies we see the world stretching out around us; we are in the middle of it; all proportions and perspectives in what we see are determined by the relation—distance, height, and so forth—of the various visible objects to ourselves. This will remain true of our bodily vision as long as we live. . . . Now just the same thing is true at first of our mental and spiritual vision. Some things hurt us; we hope they will not happen again; we call them bad. Some things please us; we hope they will happen again; we call them good. Our standard of value is the way things affect ourselves. So each of us takes his place in the centre of his own world. But I am not the centre of the world, or the standard of reference between good and bad; I am not, and God is. In other words, from the beginning I put myself in God's place. This is my original sin. I was doing it before I could speak, and everyone else has been doing it from

early infancy. I am not 'guilty' on this account because I could not help it. But I am in a state, from birth, in which I shall bring disaster on myself and everyone affected by my conduct unless I can escape from it."[1]

The short passage that has been quoted was written for the particular purpose of a chapter in a little Penguin book; and I believe that Dr. Temple himself would have agreed that these words of his describe that part of Original Sin which corresponds almost exactly with what psychologists have in mind if they speak of man's "Inescapable Inborn Egocentricity." This is a long clumsy phrase; but as its meaning is transparently clear to the children of the twentieth century, it would probably be best for Christians to adopt it, and to refer only seldom and cautiously to the old formula which is open to so much ludicrous misunderstanding.

But Inescapable Inborn Egocentricity describes only the surface of the matter. It describes something that exists very largely at the level of consciousness; or at any rate so near to that level that it could be brought into full inner consciousness by a very little prodding. The brief passage quoted above does not display to us the more "devilish" aspect of the matter; it hardly refers at all to those forces that stir uneasily and mysteriously within the realm of the subconscious, thus constituting what many psychologists now describe as "Man's Shadow Self."

The best short exposition of this whole business that I have ever heard, was given in the course of lectures by P. W. Martin, to whom I have already expressed my great indebtedness. I reproduced it as best I might to the Exeter fifth formers; and I cannot help thinking it was one of the best sessions we ever had. It really needs a diagram on the board; but the reader may build this up for himself if he chooses as we go along.

There is first a small solidly chalked circle rather larger than half a crown about a foot from the middle of the right-hand edge of the board. This represents you—as you are immediately

[1] *Christianity and Social Order* (Penguin), pp. 36-7, where there is a footnote saying that the theme thus briefly stated is more fully worked out in the same author's *Nature, Man and God* (Macmillan), pp. 356-403 and 514-20.

conscious now. In the case of the boys, their immediate consciousness included perhaps the hardness of the desk under their elbows, the fact of listening to a teacher and wondering if he were going to be of the slightest interest, and possibly an awareness of a vague feeling about something pleasant or unpleasant to be done or attempted before the end of the day.

Around this, an oval some six inches long with the little solid circle at its right-hand focus; and the oval hatched in criss-cross. This represents all the thoughts, memories and aspirations that could be brought to consciousness either easily or by serious effort. It includes, therefore, the fact of breathing of which one is immediately conscious as soon as reminded of it; it includes all academic and technical knowledge whether gathered at school or otherwise; all conscious memories; and one's hopes of doing well in the forthcoming inter-school athletics. In fact there, in the oval, is almost the whole of conscious ME.

Next, down the right-hand edge of the board we may put some scattered crosses, to represent all the other people. And between the oval and the other people we draw two or three objects shaped like brackets so as to set up, as it were, a segment of shields. These are masks; and it only needs a very little play-acting to bring it home that we all put on masks—different ones, no doubt, for different company—almost every hour of our waking lives. A convincing example may be the mask of the nervous student who took the class last year during his weeks of school practice, with his: "Right; eyes up everywhere; sit straight and look at me!" The class could no doubt spend a happy time looking for their own masks and for other people's.

From the left two large, wide arrow-shapes direct themselves upon the oval; one is chalked solid, the other hatched. These are the Drives of which many (represented by the solid) are shared with animals—sex, self-preservation, gregariousness; others (represented by the other arrow) appear to be virtually specific to man—compassion, the urge to create, the passion for truth, the longing to be whole. Both "arrows" may move us to actions morally good, morally neutral or morally bad.

But whatever be the moral judgment passed by ourselves or

by others upon resultant behaviour, the whole impingment of the arrows on the oval and the response of the oval to the arrows, is in the first instance a mainly self-centred process. The behaviour results from the interaction between the drives and the conscious ME. Whether I respond to the creative urge by patiently mastering wood-carving, or to the sex urge by masturbating, in either case there is an essentially "me-in-the-middle" kind of process. Everything in the quotation from Dr. Temple becomes relevant at this point.

We now lay the chalk on its side and draw a broad undulating line downwards across the middle of the two arrows. On the far side of the line is the unconscious; and this, it will be found, is not something absolutely unknown to the class. They will have heard of it in TV programmes and elsewhere and will be eager to understand more about it. What goes into the unconscious, and what does it do?

From very early times, since well before the reach of conscious memory, we have been taking decisions to determine immediate action. Most of these decisions were other than quite clear cut. In more cases than not, there was a balance of motives, for and against. The decision, therefore, was not 100%; maybe it was no more than 60-40. But once the decision was made, action, in nine cases out of ten had to be 100% one way or the other. Into the unconscious go the "unacted 40%s"—the arguments and emotions that pressed for some action that was not taken.

A good example, just outside the conscious memory but well within the imagination of the class, as well as corresponding to what they have seen in the behaviour of their young brosters and nephews and nieces, is that question of doing a big job in the middle of the drawing-room floor. Some in the class will probably titter when the teacher brings up anything of this kind; but if he goes forward, he is likely to be rewarded by that wonderful silence in which the more mature members are saying to the others: "Shut up you kids; don't you see he's saying something that matters." There is no need to go into detail; any teacher can describe the conflicting emotions—the rather pleasing-painful inner pressure, the known sense of fulfilment if the job is done, the fear of reproof, the memory of Mummy's praise when the small job was held for a little whimpering crawl towards the pot. But in the end, either the job is 100% done on the floor, or it is 100% held. The un-acted wishes are rejected on to that queer living dumping ground that we call the unconscious.

And so it is with all the rest. The exciting adventure that was not undertaken for fear of smacks from an erratic father; the nasty temptation that was overborn because of dawning identification with wisely loving parents; the momentary impulse to some act of kindness or creativity that was smothered by laziness or shyness; all these are thrown across to the other side of the broad undulating line.

At this point I was not quite sure about following Martin's lectures—after all he was trying to give, in a couple of hours or so, a bird's-eye view of what cannot be really mastered in less than a two-year course. For the purposes of this book I could easily have contacted him again so as to improve the piece of potted psychology that is now being offered. But to what purpose? It does not matter if the teacher does not know it all. Why not continue as I did with the fifth formers in the Exeter Secondary Modern School:

> "Now there's a bit here that I don't fully understand, and I think this is partly because the psychologists themselves are not entirely agreed about all the details. But I'll explain it to you as well as I can."

The teacher can then go on and say that in so far has he understands it, most of the psychologists are agreed that *somehow or other* all these rejects, the bad ones and the good ones, live on over there on the other side of the line. They mix themselves up with the roots of the two great drives—those pressing us towards good actions and those pressing us towards bad. And, more mysterious still, they meet and tangle with sources of power and energy that seem to be at large in the subconscious area of our being. That there are such sources of power, usually untapped, is shown in our phrase about men working, in certain circumstances, "with daemonic energy". All the inner powers then seem concentrated and released; sometimes for good as when a man works with daemonic energy in the last weeks before an examination; sometimes for ill, as has been found by sane men when they have had to cope with the "super-human" physical strength of mad men running amok. And lastly, in the subconscious, our personal rejects and these sources of energy intermix themselves with what has been built into us, not through our own individual experience, but out of the queer memories of the whole human race.

Even from this level of ignorance, it may be explained to the class that these various and often mysterious ingredients twist and tangle themselves together to form focal points of emotional power that may almost be treated as autonomous beings living their own lives independently of what goes on at conscious level, but yet with quite extraordinary power to influence our outward behaviour. When the men of old times met the more violent and obvious forms of this universal human phenomenon, they were not at all wide of the mark in speaking of men being "possessed by devils". This is the whole tangle which modern psychologists describe as "Man's Shadow Self". And this is not something that some few men have because of their outstanding wickedness or misfortune. We all have it!

Nor are those beings in the shadow to be glorified as if they were urging us to grand crimes of reckless heroism. They are more to be regarded as pathetic little waifs who may possibly behave less despicably if we recognize their existence, know something about them, and even try in a sense to befriend them. If they are neglected, or denied they will behave like mean and shabby little cads. They make a boy give the puppy a savage kick because some frustrated streak of vengefulness has been stirred up by his inability to get his Meccano to fit. They make a husband pick a blazing row with his wife over some trifling piece of domestic inefficiency because he simply can't bear the fact that he stood tongue-tied when they exposed his own inefficiency at the office. They are responsible for all the rationalisations we have already mentioned—those shoddy easily-snatched "reasons" for doing the very thing that the little "devils" want us to do anyway. They can block out memories of the things they don't want us to remember. They can give us absolutely genuine headaches on the days when we at last have to do what they don't want done. They are responsible for projections—for our inability, that is to say, to acknowledge any failure in ourselves, and for our determination, therefore, to detect others in whatever kind of fault we are in fact most prone to; and hence the words of Jesus: "Judge not, that you be not judged." This sort of projection can be seen, incidentally, in every quarrel on every village committee and on the national executive of every political party. Raised to a mass scale, it is responsible for the deadly intractable hatred between Americans and Russians.

When it is put like this, the probable reaction is to ask how we can escape from the power of this kind of thing. How we can ever be sure that our motives are pure and unaffected by the little beggars that live around with us in the shadows? As if there ought to be some trick, like taking a pill or going on a course, that would set us free! There cannot be any such easy answer. But a first step is at least to acknowledge the facts. We ought to be humbly and watchfully aware that our own actions, apparently so noble and so unquestionably right, may be distorted and even dictated by all that happens on the other side of the broad undulating line. We should be charitably aware that the same thing is bound to be happening in everyone else whom we meet. His behaviour (or hers) that seems to us to be consciously wicked and deliberately calculated for the express purpose of doing us injury, may be undertaken in all conscious sincerity for the best possible motives, and he or she may be utterly unaware of the twists imposed upon it by the queer inhabitants of the darkness. These things ought to be known and taken into account in all our dealings and in all our relationships one with another.

But they are not! They are not known and they are not taken into account when a husband quarrels with his wife; when a foreman and a workman argue about the finish of a job; when an office is set in turmoil by the boss's apparently arbitrary promotions policy; when people are sorting out the aftermath of an unofficial strike; when diplomats are discussing the latest proposal for settling the Berlin crisis. In all these cases the basic fact about man is wholly ignored; and we treat the issues almost as if there were two kinds of animal involved—on my side perfectly reasonable, and on the other consciously malicious. Even if the phrase is unfortunate in generating misunderstanding, this is what Christians mean when they say there is nothing more urgent for man than that he re-learn the truth about Original Sin. I have heard a psychologist put it more dramatically:

> "That the world is now governed by men who don't know about Original Sin is far more dangerous than that it was once governed by men who did not know that bubonic plague was carried by rats."

And one might recall the words quoted from Professor C. G. Jung on page 98 above.

Luckily this is not the end of the diagram on the blackboard. On the left of the undulating line one may have put all kinds of dots, dashes, squiggles and shapes to represent the queer convolutions that we have just been discussing. Further left one may put another symbol—a plain circle in a different colour would serve quite well—to represent . . . what? There are many names for it; but though many different people come to it from many different traditions and experiences and therefore name it in different ways, it is the same thing that they are naming. It is the core and centre, the very focal point where all goes on that is most important to Life. We neglect it at our peril.

And here I must stop offering my own version of Martin's lectures and quote five of his paragraphs from a recent article. In part they recapitulate what I have tried to write above.

> "Put in general terms, the religious answer to 'What is the meaning of life?' runs something like this. As we naturally stand, we are manifoldly divided against ourselves and against one another. The main trouble is that, basically, we all seek our own interests. We do our best to disguise this, both from one another and from ourselves. We are devoted, we do good works, we are altruistic, broad-minded, tolerant: at least, we like to think we are. Underneath, though, even

in our most loving relationships, there is me-in-the-middle, the ego-centred personality, grasping, thwarted, scheming, frustrated; heartily detesting ourselves in the self-seeking process, but caught.

"The universal affirmation of the great religions is that man is not doomed to remain thus divided against himself and against his fellow man. There is a life going on beyond the ego-centred existence. In the depths of the human spirit there is a seed, a spark, an essence, a still point, a deep centre, which can grow, become a fire, permeate the whole man: so that, instead of a meaningless struggle against ourselves we come for the first time fully alive.

"Stating it in various ways, all the great religions make this same essential affirmation concerning the life. There is in us a wholly different kind of being—the 'Self', the 'Buddhic nature', the 'kingdom of God within a man', the 'Christ within', the 'True Believer'. If and when we go over to this different kind of being we are, as it were, re-born. The life of mortality, *l'homme moyen sensuel*, gives place here and now, in this present world, to what is experienced as the indestructible life. . . .

"This process of renewal is in the main a religious discovery; but it is by no means confined to religion. Philosophy, in the time when it still dealt with the meaning of life, likewise came upon the seed, the spark, or however else the still point, the deep centre, be called. . . .

"In our own time also this self-same discovery has likewise been made. There are many different schools of depth psychology, most of them more or less in disagreement. But on one thing they are all agreed: that, together with much else, in the human psyche there is a creative process at work. Without benefit of faith, without benefit of religious experience, without benefit of philosophy, among people of good education and people of no education, among people mentally sick and people mentally hale, there is the something creative to be found in the depths: provided it be truly sought."[1]

[1] From an article in *Education for Teaching*, May 1962.

This provokes a rather solemn reflection.

For creative, purposeful, integrated and harmonious living, the crucial importance of the truths we have been describing is attested by all the great religions, by all relevant philosophies, by all modern psychology—indeed, it would seem, by almost everything except by the spirit of the age in which we live, applauded as it is (or at least sustained without noticeable protest) by all the orthodox respectable people who run it all from the top. One can even believe that the somewhat savourless quality of much of our contemporary respectable Christian "salt" comes from the fact that large numbers of regular churchgoers recite the Creed with sincerity, but would be flabbergasted if they were told the first thing about their own "Shadow Selves", and hardly know what is involved in the Quest for "Something Creative in the Depths".

How, then, can we begin to explain all this to third and fourth formers? In particular, how can we begin to show them the possibility of making contact with that "Christ Within" and of learning further Truth through that "Deep Centre"?

If about a hundred experienced teachers believed in the need and gave themselves to the experiment for two or three years, we should be able to collect from them some pretty good ideas about how it could be done. But as this is as yet impossible I must offer a single suggestion which, in fact, went fairly well when offered to a class of boys.

We take a half-length piece of purple chalk, lay it on its side, and swoosh it around on the left-hand side of the board so as to produce something which we tell the class is a fog. Without going further we can discuss the fog of moral values and aimless drift in much of modern life. Are the boys and girls right or wrong to obey or defy the order to get home at 10.15 p.m.? Can an artist work creatively when the whole of his world may be blown to pieces before this time next month? And so on. Then into the middle of the fog we draw a firm bright yellow circle about nine inches in diameter. And at first this is no more than you or me. Very well, will the whole class take it rather quietly and look down into that deep centre and listen for a possible word from that inner voice that we spoke about last Tuesday, and will they ask

> "Have I, from deep down there, ever experienced even for a fleeting couple of seconds anything that I can honestly call Me-at-my-Best? Any determination just for once to try some creative effort for the sake of a worth while result? Any spontaneous act of kindness or sympathy? Anything?"

It may be that some members of the class will actually give examples; it may be that they will only show by signs that they know what is being talked about. The important thing is, however, that we are not discussing it, or arguing about it; we are simply asking in our own hearts whether we have ever met it. If so the yellow circle will no longer represent the whole of me, with all my petty selfishnesses and that crew of "devils" on the other side of the wavy line that we discussed at the end of last term. The circle now stands for what we are asking about. And we may write "Me-at-my-Best" in the middle.

Now there are two possibilities which may be expressed on the board by lines at 45° upwards and downwards going rightwards from the circle and with arrow points on their right-hand ends. The downward line we may call: "Forget it!" And anyone knows what that feels like. The upward line must be: "Try to live it!" It is harder to get the feel of what this might mean. But may we not draw a larger circle at the top of the upward line; and then, turning again to the deep centre for answer, can we not feel reasonably sure that if we could find out what might be meant by trying to live it, then into the larger circle we might write "Worth"? Worth what? And why worth it? Maybe we don't know. Can we not leave it for the moment simply at "Worth"?

To finish the diagram, we may draw a smaller circle at the end of the downward arrow. We may discuss some of the features of life lived under terms of forgetting Me-at-my-Best—not all of them unpleasant or even undesirable simply considered in themselves. But, again asking for the answer from within, can anyone doubt that we are justified in trying to squeeze into the end circle some such words as "What-the-Heck?" And if the adolescents in front of us will take a look at some of the grown-ups that they know—decent, hard-working, honest people who never do any harm to anybody—is it not clear that this is how they are living their lives, and that "What-the-Heck?" is the end that they see themselves coming to. We are not arguing about any of this. We are simply asking "the still small voice". And if there are some in the class who hear no answer, or hear some different answer, then fair enough. At least they have listened.

But what about trying to live it—trying to live out and express this mysterious something that most of the class will recognise under the makeshift title that we have given it? No doubt the class will volunteer a whole host of precepts. Be kind, be good tempered, be honest, don't tease, be loyal. . . . Splendid! It is unlikely that any will offer the essential basis for all the rest. But if they will pause and quietly look inward it is likely that most will agree when the teacher writes up, parallel with the rising line: "Remember it!"

How shall I expect to live Me-at-my-Best if I do not sometimes deliberately think of it? The hurry and racket of the twentieth century make a noise which is a very great advantage to all those mean devils who live around with me and very much want me to forget my best. Would it not seem sensible, indeed would it not be the key to all the honesty, loyalty, good temper, kindness and the other splendid qualities, just quietly to attend . . . and may we not by now dare to use a phrase with a rather more definitely Christian connotation? . . . to attend deliberately, fifteen minutes per day, to "the Kingdom of Heaven within"? And why not attend methodically? If no better method suggests itself, what about first remembering yesterday. Whom did I meet? What did I do? Whatever it was, did it come from Me-at-my-Best? If it did, then pause and give thanks. Give thanks to whom? Never mind for the moment; just simply be thankful if something was done yesterday at the level of Me-at-my-Best. Or was one of the powers from the other side of the line taking charge and showing his face through my behaviour to others. If so, is there anything I can do today to make the bad situation rather better? If not, ask of the inner voice: However impossible to prove, is there or is there not some creative purpose in just quietly spending sixty seconds in feeling ashamed and sorry about what happened; and then, quite cheerfully, "Right; I'll try to put that devil in his place if he turns up again." And then similarly, for the day that is coming. What do I expect to have to do? Whom do I expect to meet? What chance is there today for living with Me-at-my-Best?

All this is very elementary. It has not taken us far. It has not asked anyone whether the transcendent God Almighty lives as Will and Purpose at the heart of the Universe, and loves (as nearly as we can express the inexpressible) like a Father every child in the class. Still less has it raised anything that relates to the purpose and significance of Jesus Christ. But this is correct; at any rate it is in accord with the warning of Paul Tillich that wherever the Church, as represented through the R.E. teacher, makes God and Christ the primary demand, it "does not take seriously the situation of the man of today".

If we were to stop where we are now, then no doubt the argument could be condemned as falling into the heresy of Pelagianism—into the notion that we can pull ourselves up by the bootstraps, and simply because we happen to want to. It will be said: "We can only be saved by the Grace of God through Jesus Christ our Lord."

With this I agree; but yet, while agreeing, I must make my twentieth-century theological protest against the medieval theology of some of the keenest anti-Pelagians, who seem to treat God as if He could be no other than only God transcendent. They seem to talk—(I caricature their attitude for the sake of displaying it clearly)—as if God were exclusively "out there" and separate from me so that He could never act upon me except, as it were, by something that goes "bonk" and makes me say out loud, "There! That was God saving me."

I acknowledge, from experience, the life-giving reality of precisely the kind of divine intervention that I have described in this summary caricature. But God is also within; and unlike most of us who want public credit for everything we do, He is ready to work without being recognised. If, then a teacher asks for guiet and there is quiet; if he asks children to look within and they do; if half of them dimly recognise something which, for want of a better name, we temporarily call Me-at-my-Best; and if just one of them, in response to the idea about methodically remembering it, thinks, "Yes; that means me"; then by what theology does anyone say that this has all been done "by our own bootstraps" and that the Holy Spirit has not been active in all that has happened? In some respects this one adolescent will be nearer to the heart of prayer than "Please God make me a good boy", "Please God help me in the exam", and "Please God make my husband stop quarreling", which, one fears, are about at the level where a number of good Christians get stuck.

There is a further and final point perhaps more important than all the rest. Children who respond to this kind of approach, or to other and better approaches that would be found by other teachers, will not be throwing overboard their powers of reason. They will not be accepting anything unreasonable. They will not be sliding back towards a state of childish authoritarian ignorance. They will not be rejecting any of the modern knowledge now laid at our disposal by the centuries of "amazing research and fearless interrogation". But, at an elementary level no doubt, they may begin to understand what is meant by making major decisions and fundamental judgments "with the Whole Being". In this way, at a higher level of individual awareness, they will be rediscovering an essential part of that religious attitude to Life which came so naturally, and so largely subconsciously, to our not very distant ancestors.

CHAPTER TEN

WHAT ABOUT LIFE?

THERE IS ANOTHER approach to the Deep Centre, and thence to further Truth that may lie beyond it, whose importance I may exaggerate because of its having played such a creative part in the life of an adolescent whom I know well. Even though this particular line may have less direct significance for others, we may usefully follow it as it will lead us to problems that are bound to be met by anyone who explores, with adolescents, the whole question of Life in the world today, no matter what the angle of his first approach.

> "One starts," said this young man to me, "with the idea that Reason alone is supreme. The logical propositions in mathematics and science are so marvellous that one feels, with sufficient intellectual effort, the whole of life ought to be clarified and governed by proven rules like these. One rejects as an impostor anyone or anything relying on nebulous processes like intuition or revelation. But then," he went on, "there comes a time when this won't do. One needs an answer to life as a whole, and needs it now—not some other day when the logical arguments have gone on for another half-century. Obviously one can't accept an *un*reasonable answer; on the contrary, reason must contribute to the answer one gives. But reason can't give it alone. It must come out of one's Whole Being."

These were his words; and it was clear that he was giving yet another name to the "Deep Centre", the "Inner Spark" which is the crucial point for all psychologies and religions.[1]

[1] That I have used the phrase "Whole Being" several times in preceding pages is due to the fact that this young man used it so decisively when we talked some months ago.

"Very well, then. You look steadily at Life. And as you are a self-centred animal you start by looking at yourself. What are you, anyway? What do you know about yourself? You turn your attention outwards; all your memories of family relationships; your next circle of friends; the whole little community where you live; and then, in an all-embracing sweep, you take in the whole lot; the course of evolution, all human history, and the wonders and chaos of the world today. You see it entire, as a challenge to be answered. And stripped of all its irrelevancies, it's as simple as the Gallup Poll. You have three possibilities; 'Yes', 'No', or 'I don't know'. And you haven't started until your Whole Being has given one or other of those three as your permanent answer to the challenge of Life."

If the teacher puts it more or less in these words, it may be conceded that the class will reach this stage without much of a clue to what he is talking about. But perhaps we can start by thinking of the people who have given "No" as their answer even when they may not be aware of it. They have been, as it were, "offered" the whole of Life; and they answer:

"No . . . no, thanks awfully all the same. I didn't ask for it; and now that I look at it, I'm against it. So what?"

One can discuss some of the people who give this answer, and what will they do? Basically, in revenge, they will try to take as much out of Life as they can. The leader of the cosh gang is an extreme example; usually he has a pretty low I.Q. or at any rate a low Reading Age and Arithmetic Age. The class may be interested to compare him with the boy of high I.Q. who sails through 11+, O-Level, A-Level, on to university where he gets the paper qualification for the profession in which he earns enough money to keep himself and his family very nice and comfy, and never turns his thoughts or hands to anything else. Which of the two is more effectively saying "No" to Life?

In the same sort of way could be considered those whose effective answer is "I don't know". How do they live? For pleasure? For kicks? To get by somehow and have a bit of fun?

By now it ought to be possible for some of the class to see what might be meant by saying "Yes". One cannot say "Yes" and leave it at that. After all, even if we never decide where Life came from, it is clear that I did not get it by my own efforts. It must therefore be (and this time with sincerity instead of sarcasm) "Yes. . . . Thank You." Thanking whom? Thanking what? Never mind for the moment. Let it just be "Yes" in a thankful tone. But if this is to be the basic answer, we come at once to the question asked by the man who gave the opposite answer. I am saying a thankful "Yes" to Life.

So What?

I am sure that no one can ask the question without "feeling" the answer with quite unmistakable clarity. But how difficult to find the words. They all seem so lame. I look at Life—myself, my family, my little community, the whole of history, the whole wide world, and I say, "Yes. . . . Thank You . . . so I will serve . . . I will co-operate . . . I will repay . . . I will try to make some contribution. . . ." Not one of these does justice to the answer that I felt so strongly. After thinking about it for a long time, the nearest formula that I can find makes use of a keyword from the most important passage in Chapter Three:

> "Yes. . . . Thank you. . . . So I will see how I can align myself, or get myself aligned, with whatever is going on down there."

What *is* going on down there at the heart of Life? I don't know; but whatever it is, if I can give a positive and thankful answer to the whole challenge of Life, I shall at least hope to find out what might be involved in being brought in line with it.

But can anyone say "Yes" to the whole of Life as he looks at the world today? Having lived in this bloody century now until my later fifties, I sometimes wonder: Have people of my age or older any right to suppose that the present generation of teenagers should do anything else than go screaming straight up the wall when they look at Life in the world we have made for them to live in?

It will be agreed, even by those who have not particularly sympathised with the route by which my adolescent friend has lead us to this point, that this is a question that is bound to be raised. I make no apology for treating it carefully and at length.

It is not asked that Life in this world shall be all comfortable and nice. We are altogether too tough to expect anything so soft. But it is asked that in the end the whole thing shall make sense. The almost paralysing fear is that perhaps the more we penetrate below the surface, so much the more surely shall we discover that the whole thing has gone crazy. This fear, never perhaps quite absent from thoughtful men and women, is today inflamed, or course, by the palpable risk that at almost any moment our whole civilisation—all the people, all the buildings—could be annihilated in a night. And if we are to find, when we look at it, that it *has* gone crazy, then in a sense it might seem better never to look seriously at all—better to concentrate on ourselves and have a bit of fun when we can till we die.

But would it really be better? Can anyone truly live, in any real sense whatever, on the by-product of a paralysis? Even if, when we look, we find the worst, still surely for anyone with guts it will be better to look and know than to shut one's eyes in terror—and then to pretend to live as if the fear were not there?

Then let us have a look.

And we can begin, quite naïvely, but very unapologetically, with the wonders of nature. Any third or fourth former who has never been overwhelmed by the sunset; who has never used bicycle or bus to help him reach a little stream at the bottom of a slope and never rejoiced with unlimited joy because that very stream has been flowing past that slope for hundreds of years and will go on so flowing for hundreds more; who has not looked intently at some tiny creature like an ant on a lump of sugar and marvelled that this speck of life is made of the same kind of neutrons, protons and electrons as make up a hunk of granite;

anyone who has not done these things, or any others like them, is not tough and sophisticated, as he might think. He is just dim. And the bulk of the class will agree if the teacher tells him so.

Nor is it only the works of nature. With any luck at least a tenth of the class will have been to the nearest cathedral and will agree with the teacher about the amazement of looking up the nave at the interlacing branches of a forest of trees all done in little pieces of carved stone and built by men with nothing more than their own muscles and the muscles of animals to build it with. Nor is it only the works of old times. I have sometimes asked a class to recall the first letter of their surnames so that "on the word Go", A-K may stand up and L-Z may slump their heads on their desks and shut their eyes. And then:

> "All right; sit again. Now, if you had been born two hundred and fifty years ago, then those who were slumped down just now, or, if not exactly them, then an equal number picked out at random, would not have been slumped down on their desks. They'd have been dead. For lots of reasons; but amongst others because in those days they didn't have machines to churn out hundreds of miles of the cheapest cotton stuffs; and therefore no babies had nappies; and every home in the land stank to high heaven; and murderous diseases were the normal rule."

And of course it is not only material things. We may talk about social institutions. It can be quite interesting to tell the top form of a Secondary Modern School, as if it were something astonishing that they would not know about, that they will have a right to complain if they do not like things when they go out on a job in the world; and that if enough of their workmates don't like it when nothing is done about it, they will have a right to go on strike. And when the attitude of the class, or even specific interruption asks "We know it. What of it?" then:

> "But don't you also know that as a matter of history at almost all times people like you have had *no* right to complain

and as a matter of geography, in most places today, people like you are *not* allowed to go on strike."

Indeed, the good and bright aspects of the world we live in are so many and so obvious that one has even heard the chairman of governors, in his prize day speech, suggesting to boys and girls that they, so lucky to grow up in this fine world, can hardly do less than work hard and honestly in gratitude to those who have made it so good.

This is rubbish! And it raises a tricky question for teachers: What is to be their attitude to the bad things in life?

It is perfectly easy to line up with respectability in condemning the cosh boys, tarts, beatniks, and the irresponsibles who want a huge day's pay for a slack day's work as well as the shop stewards who call unofficial strikes (so the press implies) at the drop of a hat. But what about the beastly things that are approved, or simply taken for granted and passed unnoticed, by respectability? There must be such things. We have seen that ours is a society which has virtually cut itself off from religion; and it can hardly be denied that it is hedonistic, brashly materialistic, and very largely aimless. The cosh boys, tarts, beatniks and irresponsible shop stewards have not made it this way. Indeed it would be more nearly true (though not quite true) to say that some of these anti-social types are reacting against the hedonistic, materialistic, aimless and virtually irreligious society that has been brought into existence and is now sustained by all the respectably orthodox solicitors, accountants, business men, branch managers, film producers, insurance agents and, for that matter, school governors who flourish like green bay trees and read *The Times*.

Then are the teachers to speak and keep silence in such ways that a fifteen-year-old goes out into our society under the impression that the school has said to him, in effect:

"It's nice . . . *therefore* be good!"

If so, what is going to happen when seventeen- or eighteen-year-olds come up against something in our society, ignored or approved by our respectables, that is absolutely loathsome?

Is there not a serious risk of their turning on the memory of their teachers with:

> "Nice? That's what you thought. You ignorant ivory-castled sissies. What did you know of the real world, tucked away up there in your classrooms? Be good? . . . My foot!"

When I look for my own two-word description of our respectable society I am sometimes emotionally drawn towards "It's rotten." But I cannot expect teachers in general to follow such an egregious lead. Should they not go at least as far as "It's a Mess!" or "It's Tough!" in the hope that the fifteen-year-old will understand that the school has said to him:

"It's tough . . . *nevertheless* be good!"

If this is a fair summary of his impression, may we not hope for a better reaction when he meets some item of respectable beastliness? Is there not a fair chance that it will be:

> "Tough? So *that's* what they were talking about. Didn't rightly understand them at the time. Queer fellows; knew a thing or two, it seems. And I suppose they were trying to be good in their way. Trying to be good? Them? All right; I'll have a shot too."

The minimum I am trying to say is that the teacher who has seen that fair examples of the good things of Life have been fairly considered, need not try to hold the children back when they start to bring out the bad. Indeed it would be better to let it all come into the open. They might even be invited to bring along press cuttings relating to all that is evil in the world. And while resolutely debunking any echo of the widespread notion that almost all troubles and inconveniences could be swept away if only "they" chose to sweep them, the teacher can properly make it clear that he is against many of the sordid practices that the eminent do not noticeably condemn.

Members of the class, on their own initiative, will no doubt bring up several different aspects of the cold war, examples of the world-wide unrest in which mobs stone police, police shoot down mobs, colonels bump off prime ministers, sergeants torture captives, and all the rest; at home they will perhaps call attention to rackets of various kinds, rising rents and soaring land values, take-over bids and advertisers' trickery, thousands turned off work by a silly demarcation dispute between trade unions, schools and hospitals and roads inadequate while millions pour down the drain on the latest rocket to be jettisoned as useless. If the children had been asked to collect press cuttings in the week while I was writing this chapter, I hope one of them would have brought along the report of the ceremony in which the Royal Navy's first nuclear bomber was blessed by the Royal Navy's chaplain.

It is very unlikely, however, that any fourth former on his own initiative will bring up anything relating to the deeper contemporary *malaise* that underlies all these sorry symptoms. Is it, or is it not, the teacher's business to do so?

Surely it is. For the fact is that our grown-up world has lost its way. If this is so, there is no question whether the adolescent will find it out. The only questions are: At what age, in what surroundings, and at what level of consciousness shall he find it out? It is, of course, rather a facer. When he was a very little boy, Daddy and Mummy were all-wise and all-powerful. They knew everything that he did not know, and they could do what they liked while he could not. They could do up buttons and tie bows, deal with tradesmen and look up bus times, work the sewing machine and drive the car; and even when he began to realise that his own Mum and Dad were not so clever and powerful as some of the people he saw on television, yet he still had the feeling that the grown-up world as a whole knew all about it and wisely controlled its own direction. When and at what level is he to learn the truth?

Shall the teacher help to sustain the illusion all through school days so that the truth seeps in during the first three or four years at work—seeps in, perhaps, as nothing more than a vague feeling that somehow or other there is not very much gilt on the gingerbread, the glory has departed, life isn't what it was, things never quite seem to come right, it's all rather a poor show, and not much point in trying; in fact most people seem to be pretty apathetic and bloody-minded, so why not be bloody-minded and apathetic too? Is this the way it should be?

Or should some effort be made to describe to him how things have gone adrift while he is still under the influence of a company of schoolmasters and schoolmistresses who, with all their own confusions, are still collectively the servants of beauty, love and truth?

The questions answer themselves. So much so that it can be said bluntly that any argument in favour of the teachers' not breaking the "bad news" is a rationalisation of the natural desire to keep out of trouble.

So why has the glory departed?

Of course we were once, effortlessly, the workshop of the world—from 1851 to 1873 to be precise. Now the others have caught up and even gone ahead. Once the largest area of any one colour on any map of the world was red—our Empire! Now they insist on independence. Too bad. We must adjust our ideas and our policies to the new situation. Join the Common Market; or accept real Government Planning. Is that all?

I have quoted a short passage from A. W. Watts' book *Behold the Spirit*, and would ask attention for a longer. The opening sentences recall Beatrice Webb's account of the "agnosticism, deeply coloured by scientific materialism" which has dominated our whole social life since the opening decades of the present century.

> "The opinions of rationalist thinkers," says Watts, "became in due time the common sense of ordinary people, so that today urban man is bereft of all but habitual faith in life, which is what keeps modern man from being more crazy than he is. The mere intellectual decision that there is no God cannot wipe out the thought patterns and habits of many centuries all at once. But in time a faith based on nothing but habit will weaken, and the complete insanity of the meaningless life will take its place if man cannot be

diverted with make-believe meanings—commercial enterprise, material 'success', absorbtion in political and social reform movements, all of which can easily be maintained in an era of physical expansion. Yet when that era ends, only futility is left.

"For a time, then, modern man was diverted by the free play of newly discovered powers in an expanding world. The novelty of freedom for the growing powers of the individual distracted attention from the necessary implications of rationalism. It was enough to seek freedom, and the first joy of being free made it unimportant to ask what freedom was for—save to assert that it was for a vague business called 'progress' and 'the development of one's personality'. The underlying emptiness of such a view of life was veiled by the thrill of the new sensations, which, if they were to continue to thrill, must be intensified, multiplied, magnified, to the drowning out of the ever-growing presentiment of futility. Wherefore the all-absorbing concern of urban man became business—busy, busy,—buzzing like a wasp trapped in a glass, busy to pass the time, busy just to make more business, just to keep on being busier and busier—for what no one knew, except just that *action* was a good thing and idleness very dangerous. For in silence, in idleness, there was the boredom of being alone with oneself, with that inane spark of consciousness in the abyss of nothingness into which it was destined to vanish."[1]

It deserves a second reading; particularly to take in the import of the words ". . . all of which can easily be maintained in an era of physical expansion".

A shallow faith seems to work, and seems to pay big dividends, while outward circumstances are so favourable as to allow the entire community to expand and to revel in the "sweet, sweet smell of success". Even when the cream of the good luck begins to run out, the whole show will keep itself going for a while on the strength of old habit; when this strength weakens and when the whole community begins to find that its stature

[1] *Op. cit.* (John Murray), pp. 54-5.

on the world's stage, far from expanding yet further, is tending to contract, then we may divert ourselves for a time with new sensations and the intensification of old ones; but in the end . . . and who is there of any sensitivity who does not feel the presentiment of this in the decades that lie just ahead of us? . . . in the end, either we find our way forward to a deeper faith, or we go stark staring mad.

The teacher may not be able to expound the whole of Watts' philosophy to the fourth formers. But there is not the slightest difficulty in telling them that they will soon be going out into a world where the grown-ups have lost the way. Indeed the teacher will find that the adolescents become unusually attentive when this important fact is brought to their notice. And if anyone feels that a long quotation even from an author who deserves to be more widely known, will not help very much in a row with the headmaster or chairman of governors, here are the same thoughts expressed in the adequate phraseology of Her Majesty's Government:

> "In spite of all the improvements, material, social and even moral that have been witnessed in the last few generations, *we have reached a crisis that may bring civilisation down*. . . . One of the difficulties of the situation is the confused and confusing mass of opinion and belief, the babel of advisory voices. . . . It was in just such a welter of conflicting speculation that the free city states of the ancient world went down. . . . Men are coming to realise, with disappointment and fear, that scientific progress does not necessarily entail moral progress, that men's hearts and wills have not grown with their brains, that man's mastery over nature has brought him so far little mastery over himself, perhaps not even full mastery over those dynamic natural forces which science has revealed and unleashed."[1]

But the suggested remedy looks as if it is going to be worse than the suspected disease. We hesitated about looking deeply into Life in the third quarter of the twentieth century because

[1] My italics; from *Citizens Growing Up* (H.M.S.O.), pp. 19 and 39; first published in June 1949 under Labour Government, but reprinted 1959. Charming understatement in the last sixteen words!

we were afraid that we might find it crazy; and now it is being spelled out to us that we are actually going mad!

This does not imply that there is anything wrong with Life. If in Life one does things that are likely to make one mad, and then stands in danger of going mad, this does not prove that Life has gone crazy; it suggests rather forcibly that Life is sane. Life would be crazy indeed if millions of people could do the sort of things that make men mad without *any* danger of going mad.

Let us, for a moment, climb back from the level of our present discussion so as to consider some of the more superficial world chaos that the children will have brought in on their own initiative. Roughly speaking, the evidence produced by the children will show that the world is in a mess at home and abroad. And their spoken or unspoken question will be:

> "Why? Where does it all come from? What's behind it? Why can't it all settle down? What's stirring it up? Is there a coherent answer to all this incoherence?"

Let us go back to the time chart that was the starting-point for our whole discussion. What do we learn?

Suddenly, only "the day before yesterday", and without any serious outward warning or time for moral preparation, the whole human race has been struck by a revolution on such a scale and of such complexity that there are not any adjectives in the whole language of man that are big enough to describe it.

This revolution is still in its very early days. Though it has by now shaken all men almost without exception, it has not as yet fully embraced anything like the whole human race. A very rough but reasonably fair assessment would be that about one-sixth of the world's population (almost all white) have definitely crossed the threshold into the science-minded power-driven age of man; one-third are struggling over the threshold now; and one-half are still outside.

I have a set of little models that illustrate this fact, and I would suggest that teachers might copy them and have them on display for a few days every term on some fairly prominent table or shelf. There are two plywood men; one is a stoutish white man with a suggested grey suit and felt hat; the other a thin dark man in shorts and bare feet. They are nine inches and two foot three inches high which is proportionate to one-sixth and one-half. Then there are two collapsible cardboard cubes whose sides are nine and one-third inches and five inches, which brings out the ratio between their volumes at a rough 66 : 10. And this is fair. The big cube stands beside the little man to show that about one-sixth of the world's people are now happily consuming 66% of its total annual wealth; while the little cube shows that half the world's people have to get on, as best they may, with just under 10% of the world's income. "*Never had it so good!*"

What on earth has gone wrong with us in the teaching profession when, in almost every Secondary School, we spend far more time and energy in teaching the children to calculate the areas of geometric shapes, in telling them about the Romans, the Saxons and the Normans, than in helping them to grasp the layer upon layer of contemporary meaning that is to be found in these four little figures? Is it not an indication that the Devil wants us to go on living in the sham world of a syllabus that for some queer reason has to be put over; and wants to shut the children out of an appreciation of the Life they are going to live in the real world?

It is to be understood that the situation revealed by the little figures is brand-new in terms of human history. Going back to the centuries before the onset of our present revolution, say to the fifteenth or even only to the sixteenth, there was no such difference in the standard of living between countries and continents. Can anyone wonder that the whole world is in travail while we live the lush lives that we do and they live the lean? How very nice for us, how much less nice for the underfed millions, if things would "settle down". But third and fourth formers have quite enough imagination to respond if the teacher says to them:

> "Would *you* feel inclined to settle down if instead of being born as one of the well-fed little dots that go to make up *this* man, you had started life as one of the hungry little dots that go to make up *that* one?"

Teachers could contact *War on Want*, 9 Madeley Road, London, W.5. for the booklet *Time for Action!* (post free 1/3), even if only for the sake of the photograph on the first inside page. It shows two bare-footed African teenagers yelling their heads off at a lusciously evening-dressed dancing couple on a sixteen-sheet poster advertising a Gene Kelly film called "Living in a Big Way".

Then, of course, there is the cold war. A battle for freedom! Let us come to the question of freedom in a moment. Meanwhile, are the teachers going to let the children go out into the world under the impression that our educational system simply does not know that the cold war is somehow or other connected also with the question whether the great basic industries of our new age should be owned by the State or by Big Business? At the very least, if we want to help the children to come to terms with much of the superficial chaos of modern Life, let us put it to them that staggering new powers of production have suddenly burst on mankind and that it is not very surprising if there is, at this early stage, an immense area of uncertainty and disagreement and even of downright violent altercation about the best way of owning and guiding these new forces. Far from anyone having any right to be surprised or pained by world-scale confusion and conflict in this field, what else could one possibly expect?

But yet I find that I cannot pass this point in my argument without exposing a little trick that is often played in all good faith, and usually without a single word being spoken on either side, by Conservative on Socialist teachers:

> "Look, old boy," it is said without words, "I'm a Conservative; you're a Socialist. Well, good enough, and we don't want to fall out. So don't you tell the children that you're a Socialist and I won't tell them that I'm a Conservative. After all, fair's fair."

So we are to have silence all round; and from the silence the children are left to understand that the Conservative thinks the present set-up is basically all right, and that the Socialist thinks it is all right too. Thus one Conservative and one Socialist give the impression of being two Conservatives. No controversy, and quite splendid from the Conservative point of view.

Now it would be a great mistake for the Socialist teacher to plug his Socialism as a classroom topic. But his spoken answer to the unspoken suggestion that is put to him so charmingly in this modern age of mass-produced monolithic mediocre conformity must be:

> "Sorry, Sir; fair's fair. You find some way of letting them know unmistakably that you're a Conservative, and I shall find some way of letting them know unmistakably that I am a Socialist."

There are plenty of ways of doing it other than plugging in class. Some unequivocal public activity outside the school ground and outside school hours would be quite enough. But for goodness sake let each of us do what he can to break through this "ITV" atmosphere in which we are all to be lulled into a state of mass-purchaser with the suggestion that we are really all agreed about everything and there are no more principles left to get worried about.

And what about freedom? One might almost say that five centuries of world revolution, stemming out from western Europe, have been driven forward relentlessly by all the ideas of human freedom and equality in all their many different aspects. Communism, strongly anti-freedom in so many of its present practices, is based and grounded on the simple proposition that a working man is not a different kind of animal from a landlord or a factory owner. And it would probably be valuable if individual churchmen would more often remember that the bishops at Lambeth in 1948 unanimously resolved that:

> "Communism is presenting a challenge to Christian people to study and understand its theory and practice, so that they may be well instructed as to which elements in it are in

conflict with the Christian view of man and must therefore be resisted, and *which elements are a true judgment on the existing social and economic order*." (My italics.)

May I be forgiven a personal anecdote. Estates with which my family were associated for several generations now belong to the National Trust. They are very beautiful, and I think it is right to know that the kind of building tolerated today by our present compromise between private enterprise and county planning will never take place on either of them. But some of the older inhabitants have undoubtedly rolled together all their sadness about all the disliked tendencies of the modern age and lumped the whole blame on to the shoulders of the Trust and on to those of their local agents. One day, after listening to a statement of the general complaint, I asked to be given just one specific example of the kind of thing the lady had in mind:

"Well, Sir Richard, it's all these boys screaming up and down the orchards?"

"Oh but surely, Mrs. Gammon, boys used to scream in the orchards when you were young?"

"Maybe they did; but in those days, word would have been sent up to Sir Thomas; and he'd have sent down a message to the parents to stop it; and stop it they would."

Exactly so! In the old days they did what they were told by their betters for no other reason than that their betters told them, and in most cases with hardly any more sense of grievance than when hounds rally to the command of the horn. It was the natural thing to do. In West Somerset it was natural as short a time ago as in 1905. But long before that, in the great world, Luther had challenged the divine right of Popes, Cromwell the divine right of kings, Voltaire the divine right of Dukes, Marx the divine right of owners, the whole process unleashing a tornado of new ideas and new feelings about ourselves that could not for ever be excluded even from West Somerset. As we have noticed before, the divine right of schoolmasters and the divine right of parents could not hope to be for ever excluded from the challenge.

The whole process is essentially glorious. It must be welcomed with wide open arms by all who are against the Communists on the ground of their suppression of freedom. But, of course, it is inconvenient. Everything was so much easier in the dear old days when everyone knew his proper station. It was all so much comfier to manage when people did what they were told because they were told to do it. Is it really so very difficult to show the fourth formers that they can make perfectly good sense of a wildly confused world at a moment in history when all the old social disciplines have been so recently and so rightly rejected, and when we have not yet had time to work out the new ones? Far from anyone having any right to suppose that social confusion (and rising figures for juvenile delinquency) are an indication that something has gone wrong at the heart and core of Life, are not these the very things that we should expect at a time like this? All these confusions, surely, could be perfectly well explained, even by the somewhat superficial efforts that have been made in the last few pages. Putting it very shortly: The second of only two epoch-making events in the whole history of man, has broken out into the open only "the day before yesterday"; it is hardly surprising if we now find a good deal of social chaos all around.

But, it may be felt, this has not really cleared up our deepest anxieties about Life. It might be acceptable if we could see ahead of us nothing worse than a tangle of painful confusion. But in our day we face the prospect of annihilation! Surely we cannot be expected to give Life a grateful heart-felt "Yes" when this unprecedented nightmare is hanging over us all?

One or two things ought to be said about the threat itself before we consider any explanation.

To begin with, we are singularly ill-equipped to come to terms with it because we do not have immediately behind us the tribal or medieval generations who simply took it for granted that man must naturally live his whole life in the knowledge that sudden death and disaster might overwhelm him and his whole community at almost any moment. Our immediate predecessors were the cocksure Victorians and Edwardians who supposed that they had definitively solved all man's major social problems so as to hand on to us, their grandchildren and great-grandchildren, a world perfectly fit and comfy for rationalists to live in. Each of us must watch himself for the tendency to behave as if we were all spoilt children who thought we had been promised a lush party and find we are called to an agonising ordeal. We are tempted to suppose that the world and Life must have gone bad; forgetting that

> "*if* the purpose of life is the shaping of human souls through conflict with evil and pain and conquest over uncertainty and scepticism, then this world is not at all ill adapted for *that* purpose."[1]

The other thing to say about possibly impending catastrophe is that people ought not to be so mesmerised by the nuclear threat.

To begin with, nuclear war would not wipe out all life. There are no superlatives that could describe its total horror; but somewhere human life would go on. At first survivors would find themselves pressed back to a sadly primitive standard of living. But in due time the threads would be picked up; our knowledge, our experience, our aspirations and our skills would not vanish without trace. In the first instance this is a scientific and political judgment; I have examined the facts and believe it true. But if I am pressed by the most pessimistic scientists and the gloomiest politicians, then ultimately it is a religious judgment. I believe in God; I believe He has purpose for man; I do not believe He will be defeated by any horror worked up by men.

The other reason for trying to escape from mesmerisation is that nuclear war, though doubtless the most spectacular, is by no means the only form of world-scale disaster that looms ahead. Even if some miracle could bring us a watertight agreement to abolish all nuclear weapons, humanity still faces probable defeat in the desperate race between population and food supply—largely, be it said, because the blinded leaders of several great religions still oppose government-sponsored popularisation of mechanically-aided contraception. Just a

[1] *Recovery of Faith*, Radhakrishnan (George Allen and Unwin), p. 87 (my italics).

little beyond the food crisis, lies the energy crisis when we have burned up in a few centuries all the fossil fuels laid down in almost uncountable geological millennia, and may not have found out how to produce, from tides, sunshine and atoms, about fifty times as much energy as is annually consumed in the world today.[1] Much closer to us in time is the possibility that the so-called "Keynsian Miracle" of full employment in the western world may not prove everlasting. It is quite possible that an unemployability crisis, surpassing that of the early thirties, may break over us again; and that it may bring in its train either complete anarchy or the establishment of a nakedly Fascist reactionary dictatorship. Another possibility staring us in the face is that monolithic Communism may win world-wide victory and may impose its rigid discipline on all mankind for a couple of centuries.

Very briefly, then: We thought everything was going to be all right; but "history has resumed its risky and cataclysmic character".[2]

But this still has not *explained* it! Indeed it has not; for the most important single factor has not been taken into account.

We agreed, a little while ago, that the problems thrown on to man's desk by the second of only two epoch-making events in human history, would be quite enough to explain a vast area of chaos and confusion . . . would explain it, as I think we tacitly admitted, *even if man himself were a basically reasonable creature*.

But he is not!

Now it would not be so bad if men, not being reasonable creatures, knew that they were not and took account of the fact in all their dealings with themselves and with each other—particularly with all those who disagree with them. The actual position is far worse. In total we see human and social problems of unprecedented magnitude and complexity, ultimately handled by some 2,500,000,000 animals of the species *homo sapiens*. More realistically we might guess that these problems are being seriously grappled and worked upon by perhaps

[1] For a sober treatment of this possibility, see *The Challenge of Man's Future*, by Harrison Brown (The Viking Press, New York).
[2] Professor Butterfield, *Christianity and History* (G. Bell and Sons), p. 70.

some 2,000,000 men and women; by all, that is to say, who exercise some measure of power, small or great, over public policy, or hold some position of leadership over a few hundred or over a few hundred million of their fellow men and women. Almost every one of these 2,000,0000, holding his measure of responsibility, passionately believes himself to be moved by reason alone; when all the time he is not.

I feel bound to offer a particular example of all this, because otherwise even those who know how it all applies to the personal problems that crop up on the psychiatrists' couches, may not believe that this disastrous human blindness may affect public policy. I choose for my example the senior members of the British Civil Service, and particularly of the Foreign Office; for it would be supposed (particularly by senior Foreign Office officials) that here if anywhere we should find men utterly freed from emotional distortion, deciding their attitude, their activities and their contribution to policy in the light of nothing other than clear reason all alone. Yet Anthony Duff Cooper, referring to the days just after his election as Member of Parliament for Oldham in 1924, writes of them:

> "My attitude to the League of Nations, so long as I was a member of the Foreign Office, holding strong Conservative views, had been one of sceptical benevolence, an attitude which I do not think I am being unjust in saying was shared by a majority of the civil service. Nobody wished any ill to the League, but few believed it could do any good. Here was a new piece of nonsense, created by the politicians for their own purpose, primarily to placate the all-powerful but singularly impractical President Wilson, and secondarily to serve as a smoke screen behind which the diplomatists, and especially the British Foreign Office, could conceal from the public the fact that they had no foreign policy at all. . . . I had shared the disdain with which the cold-blooded Civil Servants looked down on this clap-trap of the hustings,
>
> "When I found that the League of Nations was a live issue. my first instinct was to denouce it for the sham I believed it to be. Before doing so I felt bound to give some attention

> to the subject, and the result of my inquiries convinced me that either the League of Nations must triumph, or there must be another war."[1]

Does it have to be spelt out? Duff Cooper became an exception to the rule that applied generally to all the top-level civil servants. He became a Member of Parliament and, as such, he was led to study the League of Nations seriously; they never did any such thing. He concluded that *either it must triumph, or there must be another war*; they continued to write it off as "a new piece of nonsense, a sham, the clap-trap of the hustings". They wrote it off, without seriously studying it—without, that is to say, applying their reason to it as they would have applied their reason to a chess problem. Why? We do not know. I suggest that it was because, below the level of sharp consciousness, there was a horrible presentiment that if the League of Nations triumphed, the whole conduct of Foreign Affairs, to which they had been so laboriously trained, would be taken over by a different kind of man—by the international civil servant. And if the sheer enormity of this conclusion is unacceptable to any reader, then I must leave with him the facts and the question: It would have been *reasonable* if all these men had seriously studied the League of Nations; we learn from Duff Cooper's inside information that they did not. Why not? If my guess is the wrong one, some other queer set of devils from the other side of the wavy line of the subconscious must have been deflecting from them their clear and obvious rational duty.

And devilish forces of the same kind are deflecting the rational judgment of every senior government servant in every capital city in the world; and the same thing is happening to every trade union leader, every banker, every big business man, every politician, every statesman the whole way round the world. And not one in a hundred admits it, or allows for it either in himself or in those who disagree with him. This, surely, is the kind of thing Jung had in mind when he said:

> "We need more understanding of human nature, because the only real danger that exists is man himself. He is the great

[1] *Old Men Forget* (Hart-Davis), p. 157.

danger, and we are pitifully unaware of it. We know nothing of man, far too little. His psyche should be studied, because we are the origin of all coming evil."[1]

History students five or six hundred years from now will be as blind, of course, to the deepest needs of their day as we are to the needs of ours. But they will live in days when all the things that Jung talks about will have been as deeply accepted as are Individualism and Rationalism today. They will look back on us, and in doing so they will find the same sort of difficulty in comprehending our state of blindness as we find when we look back and try to imagine what on earth life felt like in the medieval days before Rationalism or Individualism had emerged. If they see that somehow or other we and our children and grandchildren skirted around all the potential disasters that now seem to threaten us, they will wonder what kind of benevolent Providence can have been guiding us; whereas if those students have to study the history of man's painful recovery from some appalling world-scale catastrophe, it will never occur to them to suppose that the catastrophe was brought about *by something wrong at the heart and core of Life*! It will seem to them blazingly obvious that disaster was the only possible consequence when such an unprecedented tangle of problems as ours was tackled by such blind men as us.

So now we have looked at Life and found no reason to write it off as crazy. In face of Life's challenge we cannot slide out any more with "I don't know". Just now we do know; and if tomorrow we choose to forget, then every now and then something will crop up to remind us that this will not be Life's fault; it will be that we are too slovenly to keep on remembering. Of course, if we choose, we can still give an aggressive "No!" We can still go flat out for those O-Levels, A-Levels and graduate qualifications for the job that will buy a comfy home without a thought or a hand's turn for anything beyond. But now it must be done in the clear knowledge that there is nothing in Life that justifies us in doing it. We must look in the mirror with: "This I choose because I am bone selfish."

[1] See page 98 above.

How much better to go at least in imagination—or, for that matter, why not in actual fact?—to some such place as where that stream has been flowing past the bottom of that little slope for hundreds of years and will be flowing past it for hundreds of years into the future; and there give Life our heartfelt, permanent and overwhelming "Yes!"

If anyone does this, and holds it in mind, and goes on to keep himself open to everything that might be involved in it, then amongst other things he will be contributing (microscopically, no doubt, and so that it can be utterly left out of account in terms of anything that will ever be announced on a B.B.C. News Bulletin, but none the less definitely) to the possibility that world-scale disaster will not strike and overwhelm us all in its most grizzly form. And if, despite his real though virtually insignificant contribution, the worst kind of catastrophe should in fact break over us, he will be contributing (on the same tiny but definite scale as before) to the creative forces that will begin to gather up the strings again on the other side of whatever it is that happens to us.

CHAPTER ELEVEN

WHAT ABOUT CHRISTIANITY?

AN OBJECTION MAY be made against the precise point that we have now reached. After all, we did not start reading the book to find out how to make a contribution to the avoidance of world-scale disaster. We started reading to find out how to teach Christianity to adolescents. The point is a fair one and must be treated at length.

But may it be clear, first of all, that it is my definite opinion that everything involved in the last chapter should be taught to the top forms in Secondary Modern Schools; and that it could in the end be taught there if a hundred teachers set themselves to the experimental work of teaching it. After all there is nothing in it that is intellectually so difficult as:

$$2(4x-5)-3(x-6)=5x+8$$

And it is all very much nearer to the teenagers' real interests than this piece of algebraical trickery which I have so often seen taught to them for no better reason, apparently, than that it is in "The Syllabus" and "Wanted for O-Level".

Let us at any rate take stock of the position that may be reached by someone who has been led through the proposed discussion course.

He will not be exposed to any of the Devil's rationalisations in the form: "You can't be a Christian because obviously a man can't walk on the top of a lake."

The proposed course will not, in itself, have involved him in the declaration: "I believe in God." Therefore, in examining its merits, we must think all the time of an adolescent who comes to the end of it without being able—(without yet being able)—to make any such affirmation. All we can say is that he or she will not be hopelessly waiting for a "Proof" in the normal meaning of the word; will not be bogged down, as I was, in the "certainty" that God is impossible because else they would have proved Him. It will be known that if the proclamation of faith is ever to be made at all, it will come through the same Still Small Voice that gave those fleeting intimations about Me-at-my-Best.

And because of those intimations from that Deep Centre, the adolescent, without going back to authoritarian childishness will have made a first contact with what is meant by decisions made *with the Whole Being*.

He will not go back to the grim sin-dominated kind of life that seems to have been endured by some people in olden days. He will go forward (we may hope with some solemnity) to an understanding of the fact that man's reason—adequate for chess and for making computers—becomes unreliable in the face of any problem involving emotional preferences.

And there was one thing more. We saw that our ancestors were more herd-like than we are. They were more inescapably integrated into the Life of the whole community. Of course, for them, the whole community was quite small—typically it was a score of manorial villages linked around a chartered market town. How nostalgic! Hence those who, in effect, today cry out: "Please . . . *not* a great big steel works . . . can't we have a lot of little steel works instead?" But it is useless to say "Go Back!" when Evolution says "Go On!" We cannot now shut out the complex world community so as to re-create the tiny-community-integration that was a subconscious part of the religious attitude of men, women and adolescents in olden days. Today our participation in the life of the smaller partial communities that are closest around our homes and our work, can only come as a subordinate part of our integration with all Life. Hence the positive heart-felt "Yes!" that we have been discussing, is the rediscovery, at the necessary contemporary level, of that sense of social integration that came almost inevitably to the people who lived in the feudal manors.

There is something more that has given me encouragement. I have deliberately shaped the whole structure of this book for the very purpose of finding out how we can win back, at a higher level of individual awareness, the whole of the essentially religious attitude to life which came instinctively and almost subconsciously to our ancestors not so very long ago. But I did not deliberately shape the book so as to arrive at the furthest point that may be said to be held in common by all the great religions of the world. Some may dispute that this is a proper description of the point that has been reached. But I am happy to think that William James, who studied these problems so deeply in his classic work, *Varieties of Religious Experience*, might possibly have agreed that it is.

> "The warring gods and formulas of various religions," says he, "do indeed cancel each other, but there is a certain uniform deliverance in which religions all appear to meet. It consists of two parts:
>
> 1. An uneasiness: and
> 2. Its solution.
>
> 1. The uneasiness, reduced to its simplest terms, is a sense that there is *something wrong with us as we naturally stand.*
> 2. The solution is that *we are saved from the wrongness* by making proper connection with the higher powers. . . .
>
> "The individual, so far as he suffers from his wrongness and criticises it, is to that extent consciously beyond it, and in at least possible touch with something higher, if anything higher exists. Along with the wrong part there is thus a better part of him, even though it may be but a most helpless germ. With which part he should identify his real being is by no means obvious at this stage; but when stage 2 (the stage of solution or salvation) arrives,[1] the man identifies his real being with the germinal higher part of himself; and he does so in the following way. *He becomes conscious that this higher part is conterminous and continuous with a* MORE *of the same quality, which is operative in the universe outside of him, and which he can keep in working touch with, and in a fashion get on board of and save himself when all his lower being has gone to pieces in the wreck.*"[2]

[1] "Remember that for some men it arrives suddenly, for others gradually, whilst others again practically enjoy it all their life."

[2] *Varieties of Religious Experience* (Longmans, Green and Co.), p. 508.

One does not need to strain language unduly to feel that the parallels are encouraging. "*Something wrong with us as we naturally stand!*" This is a simple general description of all that has been particularised above as man's Inescapable Inborn Egocentricity and his Shadow Self. The "real being" and the "germinal higher self" are surely yet further phrases to describe the deep essential—the Inner Voice, the Christ Within. And what about "*a MORE of the same quality which is operative in the universe outside*"? We found, at an earlier stage, that no one could respond to Life with a heart-felt grateful "Yes!" and then leave it at that. He must go on to ask: "So What?" The obvious answer, though strongly felt, was difficult to put into words. In the end our best formula was: "So I will see how I can align myself, or get myself aligned, with whatever is going on at the heart and core of Life."[1] The words are quite different; but surely the truth they grope after is the same in either case. It is not really that one thing is followed, as a consequence, by another. The very act of giving our "Yes!" to Life is in itself a reaching out to find, or to be found by, a *MORE* of the same quality operative in the universe around us.

So we start by trying to recover, at a higher level of awareness, all that was involved in an almost instinctively religious attitude to life in olden days; and we end at the point that is shared by all the great religions.

This leads me to consider the relationship between Christianity and these other religions in these confused early decades of the egalitarian, science-minded and power-driven age of Man.

Not many hundred years ago, when men and women were basically religious by nature, many expressed their religion in ignorant, and some in loathsome ways. In those days Christian propaganda was rightly concentrated on teaching what Christians believed to be the one true religion; it was directed, that is to say, towards *defeating* the other religions.

Today the situation is different. All the religions are challenged by something that is alien to them all. The "Religion of Science" would condemn, reject or ignore all the deepest insights

[1] See page 140 above.

of all the saints and mystics of all religions. There is no occasion for insight if one accepts the "implicit faith that by the methods of physical science, and by these methods alone, could be solved all the problems arising out of the relation of man to man and of man towards the universe."[1] Freud dismissed all religions—not only the formulae used today or in the past, but all the formulae that they might use at any future time for expressing their ultimate Truth—when he wrote:

> "No, science is no illusion. But it would be an illusion to suppose that we can get anywhere else what it cannot give us."[2]

We have seen already what this means: Every human problem is to be solved by an unemotional, uninvolved and uncommitted application of allegedly reliable Reason to the externally observed and objectively verifiable facts. And let no one doubt that this *is* the religion of the twentieth-century world. J. H. Oldham writes:

> "The most serious competitor of the Christian faith in the world today is what we may describe as salvation through knowledge. That is the working religion of men everywhere, the driving force of the modern world. It is what makes the wheels go round alike in capitalist America, in western Europe, in the communist East and in the fermenting continents of Asia and Africa."[3]

He would agree, I am sure, that this "working religion of everyman" is the most serious competitor, not only of the Christian faith, but of all the great religions.

Then what is today the Christian propaganda problem *vis-à-vis* these other great religions? Naturally we cannot conceal our belief that Christianity offers man a surer intimation of the ultimately inexpressible Truth than do the other religions, precisely because of our acceptance of the unique position of Jesus Christ. But is it our main aim, in meeting the other religions today, to convert their followers, to attack them

[1] See the quotation from Beatrice Webb on page 122 above.
[2] The last two sentences in his *The Future of an Illusion* (Hogarth Press).
[3] *Life is Commitment* (S.C.M.), p. 19.

and to destroy their existing faith? What about the words of Christ? "He who would be chief amongst you, let him be the servant of all." For at least the next hundred years, might it be the main purpose of Christianity, not to attack the other great religions, but to serve them by showing how they can sustain the best and deepest insights of all their saints and sages against the technological secularism that is now sweeping the world? After all, Christianity has been under the hammer of scientific criticism, in one form or another, for about four hundred years; and this hammering has now been working its effect on the mass membership of the Christian Church for a good many decades. Christianity has taken quite a battering; and, in its mass propaganda methods, it is hardly yet making use of the fact that we have been led through to a point at which the psychologists are discovering, in their own idiom, some of the basic truths that the mystics of all religions have always felt and tried to proclaim. Nevertheless, in essence, Christianity has won through. At the level of mass membership, the other great religions have hardly yet begun to come under the hammer at all. When they do, what in the name of Christ will be the Christian duty towards them?

The question answers itself.

Therefore, if we were faced with two watertight and mutually exclusive alternatives—if, that is to say, we were obliged to spend the R.E. periods in Secondary Schools so as *either* to take the children over the kind of territory that has been explored in the two previous chapters, *or* to give them further acquaintance with the Old and New Testament, then I should vote unhesitatingly for the former. In this unprecedented crisis in human history I believe it is far more important, *to Christ*, that men, women and adolescents should be taught what it means to *be religious*, should be acquainted with what is shared by all religions, than that they should be asked to gather around saying: "Lord, Lord!"

Therefore, I repeat, if the choice were EITHER-OR, I should go for the proposed discussion course at the cost of cutting out the Bible completely.

And I add a severely practical point, or (if anyone will say so) a point based frankly upon naked expediency. There are some teachers—(my private name for them is "the *New Statesman* Atheists")—who will condemn my whole course for its criticism of rationalism. But there are far more who will be in general agreement with most of what has been said despite their finding it impossible to describe themselves as Christians. Surely it will be agreed, even by Christians, that it will be better for these teachers sincerely to lead their classes towards a generally religious outlook on life, than that they should offer the Gospels without conviction. And this will be perfectly legal. The Education Act of 1944 does not say that the children must have Christian education; it says they are to have religious education.

But for those teachers who are Christians, why should it be EITHER-OR?

True, I have not held up the argument for the sake of decorating it all along with texts from the Bible. Has someone, on that account, come to the conclusion that the proposed discussion course provides no opportunity for conventional Christian teaching? Has not every educationist seen any number of points at which the Bible's message may be made relevant to the main argument?

No doubt a harassed teacher, agreeing with the general theme, will be looking forward to detailed lesson notes complete with chapter and verse references to all the books of the Old and New Testament. I do not see that such notes can be produced much before 1965 or 1966. But at least a few general pointers may be offered here.

It will be recalled that the very earliest suggestion was that the teacher would have to begin with some kind of justification for his departure from conventional methods. The revolutionary situation described in Chapter Two was to be turned into an illustrated time chart. The "stairway" from Abraham was to be brought up to date with a step dealing with the Reformation and a further uncompleted step to indicate the contemporary

"Baptism of Science".[1] Surely the earliest stages in the emergence of the religious vision become far more exciting and relevant if we insist that the vision, far from having become settled and case-hardened now for all time, is still emergent today. Under the teacher's guidance, might not the class throw some of their own inner dynamism into a "conducted tour through the prophets", if they were invited to see the prophets' revelations as part and parcel of a continuing process in which they, and their whole generation, are invited now to take a part?

And what about the prophets' message of doom?

If adolescents are being taught—or (what is for all practical purposes the very same thing) are given the impression that they are being taught—that

Christianity = Being Good;

and if the whole course of teaching, including the loud silences of some of the teachers, persuades them that

Being Good = { Learning to conform to the outlook and behaviour of respectable elders and betters;

and if they suppose they are told that all should be more or less all right for those who learn these things and do not ask silly questions; then why should they take any interest in the leaders and prophets of a tiny little tribe who cursed the respectably orthodox up hill and down dale some 2,300-3,300 years ago? But if we see that we ourselves may be facing disaster, not because of the lunacy of Life, but because we and the respectably orthodox leaders of society have worshipped false gods and followed too much the devices and conceits of our own brains, then surely the prophets' message becomes altogether more exciting. And adolescents might even begin asking, of the Inner Voice, What or Who was the inspiration of these men who spoke such deep truth to their own generation and to another generation living in an entirely different kind of world about thirty-three to twenty-three hundred years later.

[1] See pages 70 to 73 above.

"The Lord thy God bringeth thee into a good land, a land of brooks of water, of fountains and depths that spring out of valleys and hills;

A land of wheat and barley, and vines, and fig trees, and pomegranates; a land of olive oil, and honey;

A land wherein thou shalt eat bread without scarceness, thou shalt not lack anything in it; a land whose stones are iron, and out of whose hills thou mayest dig brass. . . .

Beware that thou forget not the Lord thy God, in not keeping his commandments, and his judgments, and his statutes, which I command thee this day:

Lest when thou hast eaten and art full . . . and thy silver and thy gold is multiplied, and all that thou hast is multiplied;

Then thy heart be lifted up, . . . and thou say in thine heart, My power and the might of my hand hath gotten me this wealth.

But thou shalt remember the Lord thy God: for it is he that giveth thee power to get wealth. . . .

And it shall be, if thou do at all forget the Lord thy God, and walk after other gods, and serve them, and worship them, I testify against you this day that ye shall surely perish." (From Deuteronomy, Chapter viii.)

If we change "the might of my hand" into "the marvels of my brain", the whole passage fits our situation like a plug.

Nor, of course, need every minute of Christian teaching and suggestion be tightly related to a specific Bible text. In fairness we felt obliged to consider the case of an adolescent who came to the end of the course without yet being able to say "I believe in God". But this does not mean that there will be no occasion for asking the class to consider how one might be led towards this basic affirmation. For example, we shall often have referred to evolution;[1] and it would be good, in the Religion and Life Discussion Periods, to try to bring evolution on to our side.

What about the D.N.A. molecule? I find that even today relatively few R.E. teachers know about it. They know in

[1] See pages 27, 43 and 85 above.

general that the atoms of different elements differ from each other mainly in the number of their protons, neutrons and electrons; and that atoms of elements link themselves in small groups to form the inorganic compounds—the famous H_2O and H_2SO_4—and into large groups to form starch, protein and other organic chemicals with scores and scores of atoms in each molecule. The desoxyribonucleic acid molecules each have millions of atoms; they are spiral in general shape with off-shoots each of thousands of atoms. The amazing thing is that if one D.N.A. molecule favourably encounters the necessary supply of atoms in simpler formations, it sets to work to make a replica of itself coiled spirally beside itself; when finished, the two separate and set about making four. This happens down at the very heart of life. From the single cell—the one male-fertilised female ovum—this is the basic process in the cell-duplication, and in the re-re-re-re-re-duplication, by which hundreds of millions of new cells of countless different shapes, sizes and functions "create themselves" until you get a chicken or an octupus or U Thant according to the shape and structure of the original D.N.A. molecule.

What on earth makes these creatures do this amazing job? We cannot prove that it is "God at work". And the atheists cannot prove that it is not. We can only study what happens and ask the Inner Voice what lies behind it? After all, even Sir Julian Huxley wrote:

> "Man . . . is a reminder of the existence, here and there, in the quantitative vastness of cosmic matter and its energy equivalent, of a trend towards mind, with its accompaniment of quality and richness of existence."[1]

H'm . . . *A Trend towards Mind* . . . I wonder. A process with no Will or Purpose, operating exclusively on the principles of chance and struggle, cannot be *towards* anything; it can only be *from* the changes and chances of the struggle.

Or consider the change from egg-laying to young-bearing animals. The process is stretched out over many generations.

[1] *The Humanist Frame* (George Allen and Unwin), p. 18.

At a middling stage egg-shell will be getting thinner, and the period of incubation within the egg will be but a few days. But even for a few days, the mothers who, by chance, produce yet thinner egg-shells will thereby give their offspring slightly smaller chances of survival than those whose mothers gave egg-shell slightly thicker. At this point a biologist tells me I am ignorant. I must not, he says, consider only the changes in egg-shell. There is a whole intricate complex of co-ordinated changes all going on at the same time; and it is the co-ordinated totality that gives the survival value. Co-ordinated? In each single generation co-ordinated by chance? And generation after generation co-ordinated in the same persistent direction? Once again: "H'm . . . I wonder?"

A comparable development is associated with the emergence of man. Looking tens of thousands of years into the future, *Something* (if there was anything) could have foreseen that in due time our kind of baby was going to need an immensely extended period of total dependence on parents so as to learn the many social skills on which suvival even in fairly primitive human environment depends. But in the apes' environment, where it all started, longer total dependence on "mummy" gives those baby apes who have it a smaller prospect of survival than is enjoyed by their baby cousins who learn more quickly how to fend for themselves. Once again, survival of the fittest only explains what happens if we are dealing with an immense complex of change, directionally co-ordinated over hundreds of generations, and including such apparently unrelated items as the enlarging brain cavity and the changing orientation of the thumb.

All this, of course, can only be offered to a class after it has been carefully explained to them why there is never going to be such a thing as a proof of God in the ordinary meaning of the word. If this has not been done they will assume that the discussion about evolution is offered to them as if it *were* a proof; and they will reject it as useless by proving that it is not—for example by something so elementary as: "But, please Sir, my brother says the biology master at the Grammar School is an atheist." Indeed it has been quite explicit, from the argument itself, that it cannot really be offered at all except to adolescents who have been tentatively introduced to the idea that all our really important decisions have to be made at the Deep Centre and with the Whole Being. Once this has become even so little as potentially acceptable, the teacher can take up again the question that may have been left hanging in mid air: "If you cannot prove that God exists, what makes you Christians so sure of it?"[1] To put the same point into rather more sophisticated language: What are the actual processes by which one human soul is carried from alert open-mindedness to the first foothold on Faith?

There are no new answers to this question.

Some, as William James says, "practically enjoy it all their lives".[2] Their Whole Being seems to have been so constituted from birth that they are virtually unable to doubt the existence of God. Others "catch" the Christian faith when they perceive it streaming out of someone they meet. Again there is no proof; two adolescents in almost identical circumstances see the same man or woman; one sees the Christian faith, the other not. It is rather a solemn thought that one hasty action may prevent a child from recognising such Christian faith as the teacher sincerely feels.

If one does not seem to be ordering the children that they must act on it "before the end of term" so to speak, they may reasonably be told that enormous numbers have made a leap in the dark (or at least a leap in the murk) and have found in the accumulating experience of the years that the Truth was waiting for them.

> "True? Or not true? And what to do? Dither about it till my life's end? Or resolutely set about living as if it were true? In which case, if it were to turn out untrue, what then? Or have done with it, stop worrying about it, throw it all overboard and get on with life on the assumption that it is untrue. In which case, if it turns out to have been true after all . . . *then what?* All right. Make the leap, and find out in experience if Life responds."

[1] See page 111 above. [2] See page 163 (footnote) above.

This brings us to the difficult question of direct religious experience. Most writers on contemporary Christian education treat it as something so rare as to be virtually negligible for all routine teaching purposes. But why? The Holy Spirit has led us forward to the point at which masses of adolescents will no longer take it on authority. May we not reasonably expect that if we could be just a little less arrogant in our teaching—if we concentrated rather more on the removal of obstacles from His path—it might very well be that long before 1999 an outright majority of all young churchgoers will be those who have been enabled to take the step from alert open-mindedness to a foothold on Faith by the recognised direct intervention of the Holy Spirit in their own lives.

Some people are prevented from even holding themselves open towards the possibility of such experience, by the widespread impression that it is virtually reserved for monks and cranks. In a way it is natural. Such an experience is remarkable; and of those to whom it is given, a small proportion cannot help feeling that "MY" experience must be conclusively convincing to "YOU". This, of course, is rubbish; but it does not prevent these people from racing around telling everyone about it and commanding them to join the saved. They are written off as religious cranks; and others—outwardly perhaps rather more normal men and women—maintain an embarrassed silence.

I think these others are wrong. Their collective silence reinforces the widespread impression that only the abnormal can expect this kind of thing. Therefore, not without a twinge of the same embarrassment, I look back across quarter of a century to a young man who has just read an astonishingly gay little book about God. It has not compelled him to believe; in fact, at the moment of which I write he is still in a chaos of indecision; but at least the book has shattered a stupid argument which had previously put a veto on belief.[1] Now he is lying in bed still turning it over in his mind.

Anyone who has tried to "catch" and watch his own mental processes will know what is meant by the queer feeling when

[1] See page 108 above.

a new important thought is struggling to be born. There is a kind of stirring or heaving "in the wings" and away from whatever may be the temporary focus of interest. At once all the arc lights of inner attention turn in the direction from which the newcomer is making a presence felt. Sometimes there is disappointment; whatever-it-was slips away again without identification. But this time, this which started the disturbance, strides into the lighted arena, reveals itself quite clearly and is almost immediately clothed in words of the English language. When these words are put on paper, they seem almost derisively obvious and trite. They are:

> "And if this Good God does exist, then
> you—yes, even you, you ignorant stuck-up
> fool—might be brought into some
> kind of co-operation with him."

But with that trite and obvious thought . . . what else? This is where language shows its weakness. Shall he say a swelling trumpet chord from all the orchestra of heaven? Shall he say "a mighty rushing wind" not blowing over and around his body, but raging through all the open spaces between the electrons and the protons and neutrons of which his body is made? These are approximations. But several things are certain. The whole experience was precipitated without a single physical molecule in the room being deflected from its normal physical course. The experience, even though no words fully describe it, was utterly real. It was not imagined, dreamt-up, "supposed" or confined within the mind. It was physical sensation experienced by the body. It was not self-created from inside. It was given—from "the MORE which is operative in the universe outside."

I must repeat that I do not suppose for a moment that this experience can have any decisive effect on anyone else. Despite my best endeavour, the real essence of it remains incommunicable. An approximate description has been offered only so as to suggest to other more or less normal people that this kind of thing is not reserved for special and perhaps rather queer recipients. It can perfectly well happen to "the likes of us" if we are open to receive it. I hope that teachers to whom comparable experiences have been given, will look out for the moment when it becomes quite natural to describe what has happened—in so far as it is describable—to their classes.

One thing more. Though this experience, and two or three more that I might have mentioned, can have no decisive effect on other people, yet I am not to be argued out of its effect on me. It would be useless, for example, for every Freudian psycho-analyst in Europe to try to tell me that it was all a by-product of Oedipal feelings aroused by my relationship with a terrifying father. Incidentally my father, unlike Freud's, was not very terrifying.

It remains to consider, in a general way, how some of the most important teaching material in the Gospels can be related to the proposed discussion course. And this will enable us to take up again a question that was left with inadequate answer, namely: If we say there have been no physical miracles, what is left and how can we have any assurance about anything?[1]

To answer the question we must look more closely at the process through which the Gospels came to be written. There is no argument about this today. Christians and atheists end up with different conclusions; but they start with complete agreement about the process. "Something" happened in Palestine at or about A.D. 30; and as a result a number of men and women, mostly very ordinary, worked together to build up an organisation of some kind. Those who had been in at the beginning told the newer members what they knew about the "Something", and these in their turn passed on the news to others. Some of this verbally transmitted material began to be written down and collected sooner or later; and at some time between twenty and seventy years after the initial events, four authors were appointed (or appointed themselves) and wrote up their interpretative accounts of the whole thing.

Looking at this process, and knowing what we do about human nature, we can say one thing with absolute certainty. An appreciable number of wonder tales without the smallest factual foundation will have caught themselves up into the

[1] See page 90 above.

mouth-to-ear-to-mouth process that went on throughout the earliest decades of this new and exciting little movement; they will have been told to one or more of the four authors in all good faith (or, of course, to those who made earlier written collections from which the four main authors worked); and in the same good faith the authors will have included some of these in their records.

Hence, as we leave behind the Childhood of the Christian Church, we shall no longer tax our brains to think up some reason why Jesus should have blasted a poor fig tree or banished devils into a herd of pigs. The Holy Spirit has led us a very long way since the recent days when T. H. Huxley could write to W. E. Gladstone and say:

> "The authority of the teaching of the Synoptic Gospels touching the nature of the spiritual world turns upon the acceptance or rejection of the Gadarene and other like stories."[1]

If someone likes to say that perhaps Jesus cured some poor lunatic near to the time and place at which some pigs fell off a cliff—fair enough. But otherwise, let us simply say that these things did not happen.

But what is left? If we deny the authenticity of awkward items like the blasted fig tree in this cavalier fashion, why should anyone pay any attention to anything in the Gospels at all?

He should pay attention for a very strong and fairly simple reason. Human records are full of examples to show us that queer wonder tales almost inevitably generate themselves within the kind of process through which the Gospels came to be written down. But there is something utterly different from wonder tales; something which (if it has somehow else been brought into being) may indeed be *transmitted through* this same process; but it is not *created within* the course of the process itself. This "something" is perhaps the most valuable treasure of man. It is spiritual insight.

Anyone who has any experience at all of working in movements and organisations with appreciable numbers of ordinary

[1] Quoted from *Disraeli and Gladstone*, by D. C. Somervell (Jarrolds), p. 290.

men and women, knows perfectly well that insight does not somehow come "oozing" out of their collective endeavour; still less out of their excited collective gossip about the origins of their movement. If there is insight, it comes sharply from one man or woman to whom it is given.

Then let us look at the Gospels and see whether we find spiritual insight, in word or deed. If we do, we shall know that it has been transmitted through the agreed Gospel-making process; but it will not have originated in that process. If insight is there, its presence points back to one who was its source.

Very well; suppose, hypothetically, that instead of our four longish Gospels, the only written records about Jesus were of his telling the parable of the Good Samaritan and the parable of the Prodigal Son; and of his teaching the Lord's Prayer. The two parables have done more than any other words in human language, the one to make men a little more generous to their helpless neighbours, the other to make them a little more generous to themselves. The importance of this last point might not be obvious to an "average man" of our day who manages to get by without spectacular vice or spectacular virtue. He might not know how many saints and sinners would have been left in the pit of despair by the sheer enormity of their failures, if they had not been rescued by the parable of the Prodigal Son. So, if nothing more came down to us than these two parables, what might the Inner Voice have to say about the first human author of so much good?

The Lord's Prayer is by common consent the most complete and perfect prayer in man's religious record. This is the very kind of thing that does not get itself produced some how or other out of the discussions and the active story-telling of excited members of some new movement. It comes into our record from a single heart and mind whose qualities were akin to the words we know.

Or look at the story of the temptations. The unique servant of God considers and rejects the strategies that must have failed. With the written record before our eyes it is easy enough for us to see that these would indeed be the courses considered and rejected by such a servant. We may find layer after layer of insight in what is written. Once again, this is not the kind of thing that gets itself invented by a company of ordinary people in the course of discussing the origins of the movement to which they belong. It stands in our records because Jesus thus described to his disciples, in the form of part-parable, the very courses that he considered and rejected before he started on his work.

Or simply collect together some of the recorded words of Jesus about life on earth.

> "Man cannot live by bread alone. . . . I have not come to call the righteous, but sinners, to repentance. . . . Love your enemies; do good to those who hate you; bless those who curse you; pray for those who treat you spitefully. . . . Pass no judgment, and you will not be judged; for as you judge others, so will you yourselves be judged. . . . Why do you look at the speck of sawdust in your brother's eye, with never a thought for the great plank in your own eye. . . . Where your treasure is, there will your heart be also—you cannot serve God and Money. . . . The gate that leads to life is small and the road is narrow, and those who find it are few. . . . But seek ye first the kingdom of God and his righteousness. . . . Seek and you will find, knock and the door will be opened. . . . Go and learn what that text means, 'I require mercy, not sacrifice'. . . . Among you, whoever wants to be great must be your servant, and whoever would be first must be the willing slave of all. . . . What will a man gain by winning the whole world, at the cost of his true self? Or what can he give that will buy that self back?
>
> "Blessed are the poor in spirit, the meek, the merciful and pure in heart; blessed the peacemakers and those who share the sorrows of the world; blessed they who hunger and thirst after righteousness and suffer persecution for righteousness' sake. They shall be comforted, strengthened, satisfied; they shall obtain mercy and inherit the earth; they shall see God and shall be called the children of God, for theirs is the Kingdom of Heaven."

Whatever judgment may be passed on all this by the flashy world of contemporary success, what is the response of the

Christ Within to the Christ of the Gospels? Do we know in our hearts that this is the deepest possible insight about the quality of Life?

Nor, I think, should the fact of two sincerely held and almost opposite contemporary views lead teacher and class to treat the whole subject of miracle like a too hot potato. Once it is fully realised that Christian faith or faithlessness does not depend upon the issue, one would think that many classes could take sides and debate the matter for one or two periods. And when this has gone on for some time, the teacher ought to be able to interest the whole class in some of the miracles treated as parables. Particularly if the adolescents already have a smattering of information about the working of subconscious mind, it ought to be possible to discuss with them the importance of exposing oneself to stories that have influenced generations of our ancestors—and this irrespective of any question about the stories' factual truth.[1] Teachers who are not Christians will not agree with what I say next, but Christian teachers may take hold of the miracle stories to proclaim that all through Christian history, and today, Christ does raise up the spiritually dead; He does take any tiny spiritual contribution of ours and multiply it a hundred times; with his "Peace, be still!" He does stride calmly through the spiritual storm; He does take the humdrum water of life and change it into the sparkle of wine. In many schools the children will have sung George Herbert's lines:

> All may of Thee partake,
> Nothing can be so mean
> That with this tincture: *For Thy sake*
> Will not grow bright and clean.
>
> A servant with this clause
> Makes drudgery divine;
> Who sweeps a room as for Thy laws
> Makes that and the action fine.

[1] See page 91 above.

This is true; and perhaps more than ever important when so many families have so recently exchanged the arduous variety of life on their ancestors' fields for the rather less arduous tedium of one of our modern factories. In Eric Fromm's *The Sane Society*, there is an account of how inspired leadership in some middle-sized French factories has introduced a new spirit into the work by involving almost every worker in one of a series of flourishing social units, each with its orchestra, drama club, interest groups and all the rest. It is not to be doubted that something of the same kind could be done almost anywhere today—given that rare commodity: Inspired leadership. But it is very doubtful whether industrial life as a whole can ever become tolerable until it becomes far more natural for far more of us to share with far more others the conscious feeling of working together "for Thy laws". One would expect teenagers to be interested in discussing the atmosphere of industry today.

And although our adolescents will have rejected anything corresponding to the medieval sense of sin, yet they are fairly sure to be concerned about problems of crime, evil and right and wrong; and, as I have said, it is my experience that they give wrapt attention when they realise that someone is trying to tell them something about the darker side of human psychology. The whole attitude of Jesus towards sin and sinners should therefore become relevant; and they ought to be interested to discuss the different kinds of men and women whom he warns: Those who turn aside from human need; those blinded to the real world by pietistic self-righteousness; those whose public rectitude in action covers secret hatefulness in thought; and, perhaps least remembered, those who hang around and can't make up their minds. The subject has been treated in scores of books; but I have found no short statement better than what is contained in *The Jesus of History*, by T. R. Glover.[1]

But Jesus displays an attitude to sin and sinners not only in his words, but in the whole course of his life. We usually apply our well-worn phrase about actions speaking louder than words

[1] Published by S.C.M. as long ago as January 1917.

to people whose public words are falsified by their public or private actions. But in the Gospels, the recorded actions do far more than confirm the recorded words; they raise them to an altogether higher power.

Every teacher, in deciding how to present the Gospel story to adolescents, will be influenced by the particular way in which it has made its impact on himself; and rightly so, since each will speak with clearest sincerity when speaking of that which has struck him most forcibly. It happens that this is the aspect of the life and work of Jesus that has made the greatest impression on me; I have written it out before as part of an earlier book, and I cannot leave out or re-write it here in paraphrase. The only thing is to lift about three pages of what I wrote some five years ago and repeat it almost verbatim.

If I were pressed (I then wrote) for further support for my belief about Jesus, I think I should point to the way in which he confronted the problem of evil. This problem, after all, had baffled the prophets and psalmists and the authors of Ecclesiastes, Ecclesiasticus, the Book of Wisdom and the Book of Job. It is also baffling us today when a kind of society which seemed so good and sensible and stable is running into a whole series of exasperating frustrations under the impact of every kind of selfishness and stupidity and aggressiveness both from within and without.

Jesus answered, not with a philosophical disquisition, but in his life. He went out and enjoyed himself with the disreputable and with the outcasts whose failings had put them beyond the pale of respectable society. Not only did he find their company attractive; but so did they find his. Not only did he go to them; but they came to him. Here is Matthew, chapter ix, verses 10-11, retranslated into contemporary idiom from the authorised translation:

> "And it so happened that while Jesus was having dinner in the house, a whole gang of tarts, teddy boys and customs officers swarmed in and sat down with him. A group of local magistrates, seeing it, asked his followers, 'why does he mix with all this riff-raff?' "

He did not encourage the bad hats in doing wrong; on the contrary, he inspired a good many to stop; but stop or not he welcomed them and they felt at home with him.

This was an entirely new departure within his tradition; and, I think, in human history. Claude Montefiore, the great liberal Jewish student of Christian literature, found on a careful comparison of the Gospels with the literature of his own people that a very large part of the detailed teaching of Jesus is paralleled in much of the best Rabbinic writing of about the same time. But of this particular aspect of Jesus's life he writes:

> "Here we meet a new and gracious characteristic of Jesus and to it there are no parallels in Rabbinic literature. On the contrary, a respected Rabbi and teacher would have avoided eating and sitting at table with persons of ill-repute. . . . That a teacher should go about and associate with such persons, and attempt to help and 'cure' them by friendly intercourse with them, was, I imagine, an unheard of procedure. . . . According to the Rabbis, the visiting of the *bodily* sick was an obligation and a duty of the first order. But the seeking out of the *morally* sick was not put upon the same footing, nor, so far as we can gather, was it practised. Here, Jesus appears to be 'original'. The great significance and importance of this new departure and its consequences are obvious."[1]

By contrast, Jesus could not abide the hypocrites. He offered his truth sympathetically to individuals from among the respectably orthodox; and he met others of them socially and reproved them with quiet sadness when he saw any chink of open-mindedness (John iii. 1-13; Luke vii. 36-50). But in general he seems to have regarded the self-satisfied classes as having put themselves, by their own spiritual complacency, outside the range of his influence.

How remarkably Jesus, in his life and relationship with others, forestalls the advice which our analytical psychologists would today offer to the individual in his relationship with his

[1] *Rabbinic Literature and Gospel Teaching* (Macmillan), p. 272.

own soul! However much his teaching may have been misunderstood by many, and outstandingly by some of the Calvinists, what he is "saying" to us, not with his words but with his life, is surely this:

> "Do not sin; but do not pretend your drives and impulses to all kinds of evil do not exist; do not push them down as outcasts. 'Sit down at meat' with them. Recognise them. Accept the fact that they are part of you. And above all, do not imagine that you are, or ought to be, beyond reproach."

Nor is this all. When in the end, as he foresaw, all the forces of respectability and priestly authority and imperial power and mob hysteria rose up against him, he neither fought nor ran away. I have a strong feeling that just before his impending arrest he refused a clear invitation to a lecture tour in Greece:

> "And there were certain Greeks among them which came up to worship at the feast: the same came therefore to Philip which was of Bethsaida of Galilee and desired him, saying, 'Sir, we would see Jesus'. Philip cometh and telleth Andrew: and again Andrew and Philip tell Jesus. And Jesus answered them saying, 'The hour is come that the Son of Man should be glorified. Verily, verily, I say unto you, except a corn of wheat fall into the ground and die, it abideth alone; but if it die, it bringeth forth much fruit.' "[1]

Now this was on the first of three days in Jerusalem on which Jesus readily met every questioner and heckler that the city could provide.[2] If then these Hellenised Jews, in Jerusalem for the feast, had merely wanted to set eyes on Jesus or to ask him a few questions on the spot, it is inconceivable that he would have refused them audience. They wanted much more; they wanted to take him back with them so as to see him as an interesting debater at the intellectual centre of civilisation. Very few of us would have rejected such an opportunity for

[1] John xii. 20-24.
[2] I have taken advantage of the chance of re-writing to correct a trifling error at this point. Five years ago I had wrongly supposed that this episode came on the last of the heckling days in Jerusalem.

the sake of inevitable, immediate and total defeat on the gallows.

A hundred years ago, when western civilisation seemed to have its feet planted on an ever-upward escalator, the strong element of defeat in the gospel story naturally struck a discordant note. It was largely slurred over by people who reinterpreted Jesus as a liberal social reformer. But now the scene changes; probable social defeat stares us in the face. We are discouraged and depressed. How do we now satisfy what Bernard Shaw described as "the appetite for fruitful activity and a high quality of life?" These are the very questions that challenge and perplex us in the middle of this shattering century.

Where else then in the whole of human history is there any other leader than Jesus whose whole life hammers out the answer?

> "Go on, go on. Do not grumble about your situation. Accept it. Do not flinch from the evil in it. But do not lower your own standards. Do not use the wrong methods. All the kingdoms of the earth could seem to be yours if you would bow down and learn the devil's ways. But blessed are the meek for in the last analysis *they* shall inherit the earth. And if all this leads, not merely to possible defeat, but to the absolute certainty of defeat in the eyes of the world, then nevertheless go on. Defeat on just these terms is itself more utterly creative than anything else in heaven or earth."[1]

All this, as I have said, was written some five years ago. The point I am making about it now is that quite apart from any of his recorded words, Jesus, in his life and death as recorded in our Gospels, throws out at us an answer to the challenge of evil. We can put to that Inner Voice the question whether his is the right answer. If it is, we may be reasonably sure that the story of this life did not somehow or other create itself within the mouth-to-ear-to-mouth process through which the Gospels came into being. At the end of the process the story of the

[1] *Why so Angry?* (Gollancz), pp. 98-101.

life and death of Jesus was written down as it is because Someone lived and died that way at the beginning.

This leaves us looking at the story of the Resurrection.

There can be little doubt that all through the nineteen hundred years of Christian propaganda, nothing has won more pagans to Christ than the Resurrection story. Opponents of Christianity seem to have complained that it only needed an authoritative telling of this story of how One rose from the dead, and all men (or, at any rate, very large numbers of men and women) turned to Him in faith.

This makes it particularly difficult for lifelong Christians today to appreciate that for many people—and particularly for the most sincere, the most intelligent, the most thoughtful and the most sensitive—the Gospel story of the man who rose from the dead is often the greatest, and sometimes the only remaining obstacle that prevents them from giving unqualified allegiance to Christ and from asking for full membership of the Church.

What, then, are we to say today?

Looking at the record simply as objective historians, we are almost driven to the conclusion that "something must have happened". As is said in Dr. Temple's report that I have referred to so often already:

> "Something is needed to account for the conversion of the dejected followers of a crucified Messiah into the nucleus of the Church Militant."

I have quoted in other writing Professor Harold Laski's charming judgment:

> "Those humble men of Judea," he wrote, "who laid the foundations of the Christian Church, were sustained by a magic vision which reason, because it could not enter its temple, was powerless to destroy."[1]

[1] *Faith, Reason and Civilisation* (Gollancz), p. 166.

If, at our Deep Centre, we find it more satisfying to believe in magic than in the Resurrection, so be it.

But the difficulty still remains.

Dr. Temple's view, set out in his personal introduction to the report, has already been quoted.[1] He wholeheartedly accepts, as an historical fact, the Resurrection of our Lord's physical body from death and the tomb; but he fully recognises the position of those who sincerely affirm the reality of His Incarnation without accepting the Resurrection as an actual historical occurrence, regarding the records rather as parables than as history.

If some of us feel, as I do, that for Christians the story of the Resurrection is essentially different in quality from the story of the marriage in Cana—if, while recognising the Christianity of those who would treat it as parable rather than as history, we find it impossible to take such an "easy way out" ourselves—then what is it, exactly, that we believe?

We are entitled to say, of course, that this is a question to which no individual Christian can be expected to give an answer in terms that would be accepted as exact by a physical scientist. We may say, too, that outsiders are not entitled to condemn the whole Church merely because Christians do not all offer the same kind of reply when asked to give the most exact exposition of which they are capable. The authors of Dr. Temple's report make this very point when they write:

> "Belief that the Lord was risen—the acceptance of the *kerygma* itself—is compatible both with a realisation that we cannot expect to reach clear and full knowledge in detail, and also with a variety of critical views."

Nevertheless, puzzled outsiders who are genuinely wondering whether to join the Church are entitled, in these days, to press us as hard as they can. On their behalf I put their question into the brutally crude language of physical science:

> "Do you Christians ask us to believe that every identical molecule that had previously constituted the eyes, the finger

[1] See page 93 above.

> nails and all the rest of the body of Jesus, somehow percolated through the locked doors and reconstituted themselves (apart from the marks of the five wounds) exactly as they had been before his death?"

I put it in this almost indecent way because I believe it to be the most exact statement of the very thing which many thoughtful men and women outside the Church believe that the Church *is* asking them to accept. And because they cannot believe it, they stay outside the Church even when they find the Spirit of Christ almost irresistibly magnetic.

Then is this in fact what contemporary Christians believe?

I have pressed this point, in exactly these words, on only two very thoughtful, very sincere Christian teachers. A close friend of mine tells me that he has similarly pressed almost the very same words on five or six other well-educated men of the same high Christian quality. In each case these Christians rejected the "only-a-parable" explanation; they believed, as they said, in the real historic truth of the Resurrection. But when the question was pressed upon them relentlessly in such crude, harsh terms as I have used above, then in every case without exception each said: No, he did not quite believe in it *like that*!

Then what?

Almost in passing I would point out that it would not necessarily be inconsistent with my own general view about miracle, to suppose that there had been a physical miracle *of some kind* at this moment in man's religious history. It would not be "incongrous with the wisdom and majesty of God" to suppose that the "regularities of nature should serve His purpose" except at this supreme hour in His relationship with man. I confess that I have been most powerfully drawn to this view when reading the first few verses of the twentieth chapter of St. John's Gospel; and I only refrain from deploying the argument here at length because, in spite of regarding it as legitimate, I do not believe that this view will ever in fact commend itself to large numbers of people.

Are we then left to choose: *Either*, Every-molecule-reconstituted-as-before; *or*, a parable rather than an actual historical occurrence.

I should have thought not.

Earlier in this chapter there was a description of a religious experience that was given from "the MORE that is operative in the universe outside." It was given to a religious nobody—to a man spiritually so dull that he had turned his back on the Holy Ghost for over ten years on the strength of an argument so shoddy that he would have demolished it in a week if it had stood in the way of his doing or thinking anything he wanted to think or do. There is every reason to believe that experiences of the same order, though differing almost illimitably in detail, are accorded to hundreds of ordinary people all over the country; and as we saw, most of these keep silence about what has happened because of the embarrassing fear that they might otherwise be taken for religious cranks.

In the particular description that was given, some of the phrases used were "trumpet chord" and "rushing wind".

Physical chord and wind? Science only recognises a chord when air pressures are minutely and rhythmically varying in such manner as to be picked up by the microphone of a tape recorder. Science only recognises wind when billions of billions of molecules of oxygen and nitrogen race along so as to turn the rotating cups on a wind-recorder.

Then why speak of chord and wind when, scientifically, there were no such things? Because these are the nearest available English words to describe what happened. And what happened was palpably real and undeniable. As has been said, it was not supposed by the brain or imagined in the mind. It was certainly not a parable! It really happened. It was physically experienced.

May we then raise the intensity of our consideration from the level of that religious nobody and of those hundreds of other ordinary people, to the level of the eleven men who had lived three years in the company of our Lord, who had recognised him as Messiah no matter how little they comprehended what that was to mean, who had seen his sacrificial death on the cross? Why do we need to think of physical molecules percolating through a door and reconstituting the only thing that Science can recognise as a man? Without requiring anyone to believe in the abnormal behaviour of so much as a single molecule, why would not these eleven uniquely privileged men be given utterly real physical experience far surpassing that which is given from time to time to the hundreds of ordinary people of whom I spoke just now? And they will describe their experience to others. They will describe it with a passion of enthusiasm. They will chose the only words they can. They will say: "We have seen Him alive!" This will not be a parable. It will be history. It will be the real Truth. And it will convert them from "the dejected followers of a crucified Messiah into the nucleus of the Church Militant."

I believe that such an understanding of the Resurrection would be accepted by many Christians; and that it would be acceptable to many people who are now standing just outside the Church wondering if they ought to come in. It would be acceptable to many adolescents in our Secondary Schools.

Experience shows that one must be explicit. It is not claimed that all Christians must accept it in this way. The claim is more modest. If, with Dr. Temple, enormous numbers of Christians (including many who know a great deal about the laws of Science) wholeheartedly accept as historic fact the Resurrection of our Lord's physical body from death and the tomb; if, with Dr. Temple, we fully recognise the position of those who sincerely affirm the reality of our Lord's Incarnation while regarding the record of the Resurrection rather as parable than as history; then clearly the interpretation that has been offered is permissible. It may be held by any Christian, or would-be Christian, to whom it commends itself; it need not be held by any Christian to whom it does not. The point is made explicitly so that no Christian critic may dismiss the main argument of the book on account of his disagreement with something offered in these last few pages.

There is something more to be added because of the remarkable fact that Christians and non-Christians often involve themselves in dispute about "exactly" what happened in Palestine nearly two thousand years ago, when all the time the far more important questions are: What has been happening ever since? What is happening now?

Was Jesus truly alive on the third day after the crucifixion? We must listen for an answer from the Inner Voice. But, more important, has He been alive ever since? Is He alive now? Christians believe that He has been; and He is. He is alive in the world today—the living Incarnation of the Will and Purpose that sustains the universe.

This is the very heart and core of the Christian faith. And I can believe that serious and worried Christian teachers may have read the whole book through with suspended judgment, waiting to see how this crucial affirmation would be handled. What can the teacher do, what can he say, what arguments can he use, what facts can he set in array, to which verses in the Bible may he refer and how can he present them, so that the adolescents shall be convinced of this one central Truth?

The answer may seem appalling. And yet I believe that until we accept it, and show forth to the adolescents an attitude thoroughly grounded upon it, our teaching as a whole may be in vain.

The answer to all these questions is that at this central point the teacher, by his argument, can do nothing. By what he is and by what mysteriously shines through him, as we have seen, he may do everything. But by the words of his argument . . . nothing!

Those who are shocked by this judgment probably have not come to terms with the fact that Karl Barth's theological truth —of rather doubtful applicability during the authoritarian age —has become decisively applicable to the teacher's work today. It will be remembered that we dealt with this in some detail at the end of Chapter Four; and there is nothing in all our teaching to which it applies more forcibly than to that which is now before us. After all, we are looking at the very heart and core of the Truth of God as revealed in Jesus Christ. Barth tells us it is exactly this which is not now passed horizontally from man to man. It cannot be handed to the class in "teacher's penny packet". And the teacher has not accepted this theological truth until he has stopped hunting around for someone to tell him the argument, or the teaching technique, by which he, the teacher, may hand out this Truth to them, the class. This is the very Truth that strikes down vertically from God to adolescent; it strikes through the operation of the Holy Spirit in His time, and not in ours.

This does not mean that the teacher's work is negligible.

It is not a small task in these days, to try to remove obstacles that stand in the way of the Holy Spirit. In the original and proper meaning of the word, it is an "awful" responsibility for any man or woman, two or three times a week, to meet some thirty teenagers with some opportunity for disposing their hearts and minds to be alertly open towards His approach. Everything that I have written in Chapter Six and Chapter Seven is designed to remove obstacles. The whole discussion course tentatively explored in Chapter Nine and Ten is worked out so as to promote this alert open-mindedness and open-heartedness.

If, by the time they leave school, the adolescents know that the Church is not asking them to believe the impossible; if they are not waiting for a "Proof"; if they know something about themselves, and particularly that there is "something wrong with us as we naturally stand"; if they have courageously looked at life in the world today with all its glory and horror, and answered with a heart-felt thankful "Yes"; if therefore they stretch out in the hope of being aligned with whatever may be active at the heart and core of Life; if they have been given even an elementary insight into what may be involved in the quest for the Christ Within; if they have often looked at verses, chapters and books in the Bible that are relevant to all this learning; and if the teacher then stands out of the way; is there not a fair chance that they will be found by the Truth of God?